The Practice of Ally Work

The Jung on the Hudson Book Series
was instituted by the New York Center
for Jungian Studies in 1997. This ongoing
series is designed to present books that will
be of interest to individuals of all fields, as
well as mental health professionals, who are
interested in exploring the relevance of the
psychology and ideas of C. G. Jung to their
personal lives and professional activities.

For more information about this series
and the New York Center for Jungian Studies
contact the Center at 27 North Chestnut
St., Suite 3, New Paltz, NY 12561, telephone (845) 256-0191, fax (845) 256-0196.

For more information about becoming
part of this series, contact: Nicolas-Hays, Inc.,
P. O. Box 1126, Berwick, ME 03901-1126,
telephone: (207) 698-1041, fax: (207) 698-
1042, e-mail: info@nicolashays.com.

The Practice of Ally Work

Meeting and Partnering with Your
Spirit Guide in the Imaginal Realm

Jeffrey Raff, Ph.D.

NICOLAS-HAYS, INC.
BERWICK, MAINE

First published in 2006 by
Nicolas-Hays, Inc.
P. O. Box 1126
Berwick, ME 03901-1126
www.nicolashays.com

Distributed to the trade by
Red Wheel/Weiser, LLC
65 Parker St, Ste 7
Newburyport, MA 01950
www.redwheelweiser.com

Library of Congress Cataloging-in-Publication Data available on request.

ISBN 10: 0-89254-121-0
ISBN 13: 978-0-89254-121-8

VG
Cover and text design by Phillip Augusta.
Cover art titled *Maklala* by Chris Augusta, copyright © 2006.
Typeset in Bembo
Printed in the United States of America
12   11   10   09   08   07   06
7   6   5   4   3   2   1

The paper used in this publication meets the minimum requirements of the
American National Standard for Information Sciences—Permanence of Paper
for Printed Library Materials Z39.48–1992 (R1997).

This book is dedicated to Ginny Jordan,
without whose generous support in so many areas
it would never have been written

Contents

Acknowledgments

I would like to thank Linda Vocatura for her continuing support and her contribution to all of my ideas. I would also like to thank my meditation group for supporting me through sickness and health. A special thanks to my publisher, whose kindness in working with me under difficult conditions I value greatly. And to my family and all the friends and colleagues who made their feelings known to me when I needed them most.

PART I

The Theory of Ally Work

If then you not make yourself equal to God, you cannot apprehend God; for like is known by like. Leap clear of all that is corporeal, and make yourself grow to a like expanse with that greatness which is beyond all measure; rise above all time, and become eternal; then you will apprehend God. Think that for you too nothing is impossible; deem that you too are immortal, and that you are able to grasp all things in your thought, to know every craft and every science; find your home in the haunts of every living creature; make yourself higher than all heights, and lower than all depths; bring together in yourself all opposites of quality, heat and cold, dryness and fluidity; think that you are everywhere at once, on land, at sea, in heaven; think that you are not yet begotten, that you are in the womb, that you are young, that you are old, that you have died, that you are in the world beyond the grave; grasp in your thought all this at once, all times and places, all substances and qualities and magnitudes together; then you can apprehend God.
　　　　　　　　　—*Corpus Hermeticum,*
　　　　　in Brian Copenhaver, ed., *Hermetica*

CHAPTER I
_____

Introduction

All gods reside in the world of the imagination. Indeed, the world of the imagination holds all demons as well. To say this, however, is to no way imply that gods and demons are unreal; quite the opposite. There is no place more real than the imagination. In it we encounter the truth of our souls, and what could be truer than this? The lies we tell ourselves in ordinary life are burned away by the sun of vision and insight when we cross the border into the imaginal.

There are many reasons to make the quest into the imagination; yet the one I found the most compelling was to find my divine partner, twin of my soul, whom I have called "the ally." An ally is a divine being, a face of God that is unique to each human being. Every one of us has an ally with whom we could live, but of course most people are not aware of this fact, largely because they have been cut off from the imagination. Most Westerners are estranged from the imagination because our culture decided centuries ago to emphasize the material world and its reality to the detriment of the imaginal. Even our religious leaders abandoned the imagination in favor of dogma and doctrine. The very source of religious inspiration and vision was denied to all but a saintly few, and even these few were carefully controlled, lest their visions suggest any truth other than the accepted ones. Insight and revelation were denied to the present and reserved for the past, where the visionaries of the day were "safely" buried and could cause no problems for the status quo.

It is depressing to read the history of the imagination in our culture. There is an old Gnostic myth that the great goddess of wisdom, Sophia, was captured and held in bondage by the forces of evil. Though she is the great goddess in her own realm, she remains in bondage in ours. What is true of Sophia is true of the imagination. It is the source of extraordinary experience and wisdom and yet it remains imprisoned in our world—as if the evil Archons of the Gnostic myth still reign and keep all power for themselves by denying true vision to any but their own. In the same Gnostic myth, Sophia came to Eve in the Garden of Eden as the serpent, urging her to awaken to true knowledge. She still comes to us in our dreams with the same message: Awaken to yourself and discover who you really are.

We are gradually responding to Sophia's call and are daring to partake of the forbidden fruit of personal revelation and truth. We do so by entering once more (as in "pagan" days, long ago) the illicit landscape of the imaginal. Many of us who do find not only a personal truth, but also the presence of a personal God unique to each of us. When we first make contact with this personal deity, it often remarks: Where have you been?

Where, indeed? We have been lost in the illusion of our aloneness, convinced that we alone are real, while we suppose that if spirit has any reality to it at all, it awaits us in the world to come. As for the here-and-now, this world hovers on the brink of disaster, worshipping, if anything at all, an invisible and unknowable deity. Because we have no intimate contact with the divine, we must rely on scripture and on those who interpret it for us. Much of mainstream spirituality involves reading sacred text not as symbol but as literal truth. This form of spirituality requires neither imagination nor commitment to uniqueness; faith and rigorous devotion to a truth that revealed itself once and which tolerates neither additions nor subtractions constitute its basic foundation. All too often the doctrine of such a static form of spirituality sets its followers to struggle with others who do not conform to their principles. Truly we live in a world in which the imagination lies impoverished.

The well of the imaginal has not gone dry, however. Rather, it is that few bother to draw water from it. If we did, we would discover that, with a little effort, we could drink deeply from that water and refresh our soul in a remarkable way. More people today are recognizing their inner aridity and, wishing to quench their thirst, simply do not know how. Part of the consequences of the current spiritual poverty is that there are few capable teachers in a position to introduce others to the imaginal realm. This lack of teachers discourages people who otherwise might seek to find their way to the imaginal world, and confuses those who do try.

There are many books today on the topic of spiritual practice and many good introductions to inner practice, but few either deal with the ally or encompass a sustained practice. In this book, I offer a series of practices by which an individual can create and develop an on-going relationship with his or her ally. I have a unique ability to present this material as I have been in relationship with an ally for forty years. During this time, I have had many experiences of the imaginal realm that have taught me a great deal about how to work with an ally. I have also presented hundreds of workshops and classes on the ally and practices related to working with an ally. Over the years I have used these practices many times both in my own ally work and in teaching others. It has been my experience that individuals who continue to work these practices on their own are successful in developing a healthy and enriching relationship with their allies.

In addition to my own experiences, I have consulted a tradition which, through the centuries, retained a commitment to the imaginal. This tradition, known today as the Western mystery tradition, includes alchemy, Gnosticism, Sufism, and the Kabbalah. The present work is not a theoretical study but a practical guide, so I do not include a great deal of theoretical discussion. I have sprinkled comments and examples from these traditions throughout the book to illustrate my points and to clarify some of the practices. I make no attempt to explain these schools of thought in detail, nor do I correlate their ideas with my own. I believe, however, that ally work has much in common with all of them and find in them much useful instruction. In particular, the symbols of the alchemical path are valuable for understanding ally work, and I will primarily use these images to explain the nature of this work. For this reason, I will discuss alchemy at greater length than the other traditions.

Ally work is not for everyone, as no path can be. I shall describe the nature of ally work during the remainder of this introduction. If you find ally work appealing and wish to explore this avenue of spiritual development, I recommend that you read further and experiment with the practices described in the rest of the book.

The Ally

Sufi mystics centuries ago puzzled over the uniqueness of the human being. They believed that uniqueness was one of the most significant attributes of human existence. If this is so, they wondered, is it likely that God or the Holy Spirit—the agent responsible for religious inspiration and prophecy—would only offer universal truths? They supposed that it was in fact much more likely that both God and the Holy Spirit would provide individual revelations to correspond with the uniqueness of the person receiving the revelation. If we accept the Sufi premise, it is possible to imagine a spiritual teaching that encourages each individual to seek his or her own revelation of truth and relationship to God. It would hold that truth is not singular but multi-faceted and that no one person or faith has the right to deny another's revelation. If we could all accept such tenets, it is inconceivable that religious warfare and hatred would continue, or that one faith would use force to impose itself on another. We need only remember how many millions of people died in the name of a religion that proclaimed itself as the only true way to realize what a vast improvement belief in uniqueness would be.

Instead of fanatical faith in one truth, the Sufis discovered that the only universal truth is that all revelation is unique. They learned that God reveals Itself to those who experience It as a being with many faces and forms. They also discovered that there was one face for each person, and that by revealing Itself in this way, God manifested every aspect of Its being. The great Sufi mystic Ibn Arabi expressed the diversity of revelation in this way:

> The divine effusion is vast, because He is vast in bestowal. There is no shortcoming on His part. But you have nothing of Him except what your essence accepts. Hence your own essence keeps the Vast away from you and places you in the midst of constraint. The measure in which His governance occurs within you is your "Lord." It is He that you serve and He alone that you recognize. This is the mark within which He will transmute Himself to you on the day of resurrection, by unveiling Himself. In this world, this mark is unseen for most people. Every human being knows it from himself, but he does not know that it is what he knows.[1]

In other words, God is infinite but reveals Itself to an individual as Lord for that individual. The truly wise person knows all the aspects of God, but each individual has a mark of the divine or an aspect of the Divine that belongs to him or her eternally. This mark can be the God of an organized religion or one unique to the individual. It is as if God wishes to grow as a unique being in the soul of each individual, because it is the individual alone who can manifest the diversity that is God. The unique face of God that comes as a living being to unite with a particular person is what I call the ally.

Many years ago, I encountered my individual revelation of God. Long before I knew anything about spiritual practice, I struggled to be in relationship with this entity whom I experienced as deeply loving and whom I in turn loved. Later, when I began to speak about such experiences, I discovered that many people had encountered allies as well, but, for the most part, did not know how to understand their experience. I began to use the word "ally" for this individual God because I was very interested in Shamanism. I was not, and still am not, satisfied with this word, and often sought a substitute, but with no success. It is therefore important to note that I use the word in a different sense than is usual for Shamanism. I define the ally as a divine being who appears in the imaginal realm to partner with a specific individual. It awaits its partner for as long as necessary and never seeks another. It is paired with only one human and so must wait for its partner to seek it. If its partner never seeks union, then the ally remains alone and unfulfilled.

The ally was known to the esoteric tradition and the Sufis in particular developed the concept of Perfect Nature, or the Angel of one's Being. A great Sufi sage, Suhrwardi, spoke of this angel as follows:

> This is why the ancient Sages . . . initiated into things the sensory faculties do not perceive, maintained that for each individual soul, or perhaps for several together having the same nature and affinity, there is a being in the spiritual world which throughout their existence watches over this soul and group of souls with especial solicitude and tenderness, leads them to knowledge, protects, guides, defends, comforts them, leads them to victory; and this being is what they called Perfect Nature; This friend, defender and protector is what in religious terminology is called the Angel.[2]

There are many types of imaginal figures, but the ally is unique and has special characteristics. In order to do ally work, a person has to meet his or her ally and differentiate it from other imaginal beings. With a little preparation and practice, this is not so hard to do. The ally appears as a loving and accepting companion. People often say that, from the first, they loved and were loved by the ally. For others the love takes time to manifest, but in all cases it is part of the relationship. In the same way, the ally is completely accepting of its partner, though not afraid to ask for change when necessary. One woman said that in her first experience with the ally, she felt as if she had been "seen" for the first time in her life. Many people speak of the ally in this way and often add that the ally welcomed them as a long-lost friend. One client had a dream about returning to his high school and opening his locker some twenty years after graduating. As he opened the door, a baby tiger leapt into his arms and said, "I've been waiting for you." Since the ally is eternally awaiting its partner, it is no wonder that it acts as if it had been expecting him.

Almost from the first, the ally greets us with such joy and love that it is hard to mistake it for anything else. No other imaginal being meets us in this way. It is possible to feel the yearning of the ally to engage in partnership and to begin its journey of transformation. It not only loves its partner, it needs him or her and often says so. It needs its partner's love and attention, for without that attention it remains stunted and undeveloped. It requires relationship above anything else, and this differentiates it from other imaginal beings that have different agendas. Moreover, the relationship that it craves is one between equals. It does not seek worshippers or devotees, but partners. As partners, the individual and the ally help each other grow. The more developed or individuated a human, the more the ally manifests, as if the ally must await a large enough consciousness to unite with before it can fully manifest. The ally therefore encourages the growth of its partner. Despite the expectations of many partners, the ally does not remove problems or make life simple and easy; rather, it encourages growth and development and helps its partner meet challenges, not avoid them. It is not a magic genie that grants wishes, but a loving companion that helps bring about transformation and wholeness. In return, it asks its partner to help it transform and become whole as well.

The love that exists between the ally and its partner is like no other love and seems to include all other types of love. As Henry Corbin wrote of the mystical thought of Avicenna, "the love that exists between the angelic Intelligence and the soul is compared not only to the affection between parent and child, between master and disciple, but to the reciprocal love of lovers."[3] The angelic Intelligence is identical to the ally, so one might say that the love between the ally and its friend includes all other forms of love but is not identical to any of them.

The ally has other special characteristics as well. When it appears to its partner, he or she may be struck by a peculiar feeling of power, presence, and wisdom. The ally can also create a sense of the numinous; as an entity that embodies the divine energies and essences, its partner instantly "knows" it to be a god. Despite this divine grandeur, the ally never loses its desire to be a partner. Yet the very fact of its presence creates transformation and growth and we can imagine our self being carried on the path toward wholeness.

The ally not only creates growth but it grows itself. Most imaginal figures lose energy the more we work with them, so that, after a time, they disappear or are replaced by other figures. The ally, on the other hand, grows stronger the more we work with it, and it never disappears. You may wonder how an ally grows or develops. It gains in consciousness, in the capacity to incarnate in the imaginal, and it shines with a brighter light. Though it is capable of infinite growth, it always remains true to itself. People often ask me if the ally can assume many forms or if it always stay in one. It can alter its form depending on the situation, but it always retains a certain "feel" so that we always recognize our ally in whatever form it has assumed.

The ally is a unique divine being filled with potential for development. It appears to its partner as soon as the partner seeks relationship with it. It manifests in the imaginal and can often appear spontaneously. However, it rarely appears more than once unless its partner works with it because it needs the partner's help in order to manifest and communicate. In order to help it, the partner must learn how to access the imagination.

Alchemy

Though the current situation of the imagination in our culture is bleak, this has not always been the case. Other traditions, formed in earlier times, respected the imagination and gave it a place of honor. Their understanding of and work with the imagination remains a source of great information today. Of these traditions, alchemy has been my favorite and the subject of all my previous books. I find in the symbolism of alchemy an invaluable guide to the imaginal worlds and a map for ally work that portrays the process by which one can come into union with the ally.

Often depicted as either a fraudulent belief in the possibility of making gold from other metals, or a proto-chemistry that gave birth to the science of chemistry, alchemy is actually a mystery tradition that teaches initiates the path to spiritual transformation. Much of the mystery taught by the alchemists remains unknown or obscure, but a careful study of the symbols reveals a great deal. All who study alchemy today are indebted to the pioneering work of C. G. Jung. It is not always possible to agree with his conclusions, but his methodology remains of supreme importance in working with alchemy.

Jung demonstrated that a careful study of the symbols found in alchemical treatises reveals the process of individuation through which the psyche transforms and the Self becomes manifest. The same symbols disclose much about imaginal reality and ally work. I discuss alchemical imagery to construct a context in which the practical exercises of ally work can most fully be understood.

Alchemy concerns itself primarily with the creation of a magical instrument of transformation known as the Philosopher's Stone. This Stone has many attributes that relate it to the ally. The creation of the Stone therefore parallels the creation of the ally through ally work. In chapter one, when I discuss the beginning search for the ally, I shall outline the parallels between the Stone and the ally. If we accept the analogy between these two, we can use the alchemical processes to guide us in our ally work, for the same processes that in alchemy give birth to the Stone do so for the ally in ally work. Alchemy consists of archetypal images and processes, so the great value in studying alchemy is that it reveals insights that apply to many other processes, such as that of individuation. To give birth to the ally in your soul does not require that you be an alchemist, but you can use the symbols of alchemy to guide you into the imaginal processes through which you can help bring the ally to birth. From the perspective of the imaginal, alchemy has little to do with cooking and smelting, but a great deal to do with inner processes.

By using the images alchemy provides for these inner processes, I have constructed a way of understanding certain practices and the role they play in ally work. These practices accomplish in the psyche the essential purpose of alchemy—transformation and incarnation. As I shall show, it is not only the human partner who transforms in the course of ally work, but the ally as well. There are very real processes and experiences that occur in conjunction with the practices spelled out later in this book, and these processes relate closely to the processes described in alchemy. The comparison between alchemy and ally work is not merely symbolic, for both deal with actual processes that one must experience if one hopes to gain the final prize. In ally work as well as in alchemy these processes take place in the strange realm called the imaginal.

The Imaginal Realm

Those who have read my earlier books recall that I spoke of the psychoid world to denote the reality of beings who belong neither to the ordinary world nor to the world of the unconscious. These beings are autonomous, real entities who are not part of the psyche but have their own domain. To differentiate their realm from that of the psyche, I termed it psychoidal. I preferred the term psychoid to imaginal because people bring so many associations and reactions to the word "imagination" that I hoped to avoid people prejudging the nature of ally experiences. However, I now place the psychoid within the imaginal realm, as a special case of imaginal experience. Ally experiences take place in the imaginal realm, along with many other experiences, from that of UFOs to visions of the Virgin. I think of the imaginal as a place of experience in which nonordinary perceptions occur. It is possible to create a way to categorize these experiences, keeping in mind that all belong to the imaginal.

In keeping with this view, I define *imagination* as the faculty that perceives imaginal reality, in which dwell imaginal beings of all kinds, including the ally. The imaginal space is the place in which conscious, but not physical, entities put on form and appear with shape, substance, and definable attributes. Spiritual entities who exist beyond the ordinary world communicate with us by assuming form in the imaginal. We can perceive them through the imagination and engage in a relationship which would not be possible if they did not enter the imaginal. Such entities enter the imaginal from above, as it were, and humans enter it from below and they meet in the middle or imaginal space.

There are parallels to this conception of the imaginal in the writings of the Sufis. In particular, Ibn Arabi tried to explain the nature of the imaginal and imaginal beings and offered some fascinating ideas. I will only mention a few that help clarify my ideas.

In the first place, Ibn Arabi believed that the imagination belonged only to the soul. It is the ability of the soul that "embodies meaning by thinking and understanding in appropriate concepts and images and which spiritualizes the bodily and sensory realm by bringing images of concrete, external realities into the soul by way of the senses."[4] In other words, imagination brings higher meaning of the spirit into the soul and raises lower, concrete reality to the soul through the creation of images. It is a supreme way of knowing reality and completely free, for it possesses "complete free acting."[5] At the same time, the spirit becomes "corporealized to eyesight through imagination" while imagination is the "earth of reality."[6]

Imagination is real and brings into union the three dimensions of reality: soul, body, and spirit. Belonging to the soul, it allows us to perceive spirits that are embodied in the imaginal world, or the world of reality. By saying these spiritual beings assume form, I do not mean that they always appear as images, for they could make themselves known through feeling, or what I call the felt sense. The felt sense is the ability to perceive imaginal reality directly, in a special way without using the other senses, such as sight or hearing; it acts as a sixth sense. While the felt sense is not the only way we may work with the imagination, it is an important addition to the usual way we perceive. Since many of the practices in this book serve to increase the felt sense, I shall speak of it more in later chapters. I only wish to mention it now to point out that imagination does not always become activated with images.

Using the imagination means that you employ a special capacity to experience imaginal realities. Far from being something made up or unreal, imagination is the perception of a higher reality, one closer to the spiritual world. In this sense, to be imaginative does not mean that you are clever at making things up or seeing possibilities, but rather that you possess skill in perceiving the imaginal. To develop your imagination is to cultivate the capacity to see and relate to imaginal beings. Everyone experiences imaginal spaces, for everyone dreams, but learning to perceive this space while awake is not easy. It is the purpose of this book to provide practices that develop imaginative skills so that you will be able to perceive the ally. In addition, these practices also teach you how to create a union with the ally.

While it is useful to conceive of imaginal space as a whole, it is also possible to differentiate within the imaginal. I believe that there are two central criteria by which we may differentiate imaginal space. The first is what I call *the objective level of the experience*. I mentioned earlier that we can experience the imaginal without perceiving form, for we can feel what has occurred without necessarily seeing it. By "objective level of experience," I refer to a continuum on which all imaginal encounters might be placed. This continuum begins with experiences that are not tangibly real. You may have an inner image or a fleeting vision of a being. You will probably sense that these encounters do not feel "real" in the way that outer, objective reality does. This by no means implies that the experience is unreal, for it is meaningful and has actually occurred. But it has occurred in the imaginal space not far from the individual consciousness, so the experience is not objectively compelling.

At the other end of the continuum lie experiences that have all the objective characteristics of outer reality. Here, you find yourself transported to another space, for example, and that space is completely real. You can feel it, touch it and smell it, but you know all the same that it is not part of ordinary reality. I once awoke in the middle of the night to find myself simultaneously at home in bed and on top of a mountain. The mountain was completely real to me; I felt the cold, the hard rocks, and even a wave of vertigo as I gazed down, but I also knew I was at home in bed and that this mountain was not in normal time and space. This experience, though imaginal, was objectively real, as real as the outer world. I do not like to use the word "real" because all imaginal experiences are real. Nevertheless there is a qualitative difference in the objective way the experience presents itself. As a general rule, the more seemingly real the experience, the more profound the impact. All imaginal experiences are real and possess meaning; we can, however, differentiate them along the axis of objectivity.

In Kabbalistic tradition, there are several mystics who refer to the participation of the senses in imaginal experience. Rabbi Joseph ben Shalom Ashkenazi, in the late 13th century, wrote:

> . . . he will see with his imaginative faculty with all the organs of sight, and he will smell with all the organs of smell, and he will taste with all the organs of taste, and he will touch with all the organs of touch, and he will walk and levitate.[7]

It must be emphasized, however, that objective reality may occur without images or sensory data. You may have an imaginal experience that has the quality of complete reality, without seeing or hearing anything. You may feel drawn into a wave of light, for example, but can understand nothing of the experience in terms of normal senses; yet the experience is objectively real. Clearly, this criterion is not absolute or completely accurate, but is meant only to give a perspective on the nature of the experience.

The second criteria for differentiating the imaginal experience has to do with *the felt sense* I mentioned previously. There is really no word in English that expresses what I mean by this phrase. This is the sense that comes most alive in imaginal space and it involves a direct knowing and intense feeling. "Feeling" in this case does not refer to emotion but to the intensity of an experience. We can all remember experiences that stand out because of the intensity with which we underwent them. These are the special moments—good and bad—in our lives. By "direct knowing," I specifically mean that we feel/sense the nature of an imaginal being. We know what their nature is, what their intentions are, and what their words really mean. A figure appears, for example, and you know immediately that she is a feminine being with good intentions, even though no word has yet been exchanged. If you question how you know such things it is impossible to answer except to say that you just know. The more such felt awareness occurs in an imaginal experience, the more real and powerful the experience. The degree and quality of felt experience therefore serves as a way of evaluating the nature of the imaginal experience.

Often, but not always, the objective perceptual experience increases as the felt experience intensifies. An experience that combines a high level of felt experience with clear, objective reality forms the most profound of imaginal states. There are any number of possible combinations of these variables determining the nature of the imaginal condition. Considering these combinations allows you to determine the depth of the experience and, most importantly, where you need to focus more effort. For example, a person who has trouble experiencing a felt sense will not have a high level of objective experience either, so she would be well advised to attempt to improve her felt sense. A person who has a strong felt sense but rarely objective perception would work on improving the latter.

People often complain that their ally does not speak or they cannot feel it deeply, and suggest that the ally should do something about it. Some even think that lack of deeper experiences indicates a failing on their part, as if they were incapable of having such experiences. Most often, a little practice with the right intention improves the quality of their experience dramatically. Many of the practices I designed are geared toward improving these two most important factors in imaginal experiences. Like everything else, imaginal work improves with practice. While all imaginal experiences have meaning, there is no doubt that the deeper the experience the more profound the impact on the psyche, and, in some ways, the more satisfying the interaction with the ally. It is important to approach the possibility of improving your visionary capacity with patience and resolve, the very qualities you will need in the performance of ally work as a whole.

The Nature of Ally Work

Ally work is the conscious effort to form and maintain a relationship with your ally. The ally participates in this work as well, but ally work refers mainly to the effort of the human partner toward relationship. Forming a deep and lasting union with the ally is not easy. It requires much effort and rarely occurs without that effort. Those who make the greatest effort have the greatest success.

There are differences in the ability with which people begin ally work. Some people are gifted in imaginal processes and quickly meet and dialogue with the ally, while others are slow to start and have trouble encountering the ally. Regardless of your initial gift, if you work at it, you will deepen your experience and relationship. I have witnessed people who never believed they could meet the ally struggle for years, when suddenly the relationship blossomed into an exciting, nourishing union. I have never observed failure to reach the goal with prolonged effort, but I certainly have seen people for whom the work began easily flag and quit when the going got rough. Success or failure at creating an ally relationship depends neither on talent nor fate, but on desire and effort.

The alchemists were also aware of what was required to create the Philosopher's Stone. They warned that all impatience was "of the devil." As the teacher Morienus says:

> And the very root of this knowledge is to act with care and perception at the time of composition, avoiding all haste and error, and watching patiently day and night. . .[8]

Those doing ally work also need this care and perception with the avoidance of all haste. Knowing the value of the goal and having the desire to reach it will help you maintain steady progress.

The ally offers an inexhaustible supply of love to its partner, but it requires attention in return. The partner must be willing to pay attention to the ally through dialogues and other forms of active imagination because it is through these that the ally grows. The partner demonstrates his or her love through the simple and concrete step of spending time with the ally, and of turning his or her thoughts to the ally frequently. This forms the bulk of ally work, but there are variations in the way the partner attends.

I have discussed the felt sense and the objective level of the experience. The more profound these two criteria of imaginal experience are, the more profoundly is the partner affected by the experience. However, the ally also benefits from an increased ability on its partner's part to imagine. The stronger the felt sense and the more objective reality, the stronger the ally grows from your attention. Increasing your skill not only improves the depth of your experience, but nourishes the ally more completely. Ally work includes all the practices and processes by which your ability to imagine improves.

Ally work also aims at uniting the ally with its partner. Alchemy provides several models by which one may understand the nature of this union, and we will briefly examine one of them.

The goal of alchemy is to create the Philosopher's Stone, which corresponds to the creation of a permanent, ongoing, and transformative union between the ally and its partner. Understanding the overall process and the function of the practices in the process brings into focus the importance of the particular practices as well as giving a rough map of the work.

Many alchemists break down the total process of creating the Stone into three main parts, each of which corresponds to a particular form of relationship between the alchemist and the stone, as well as between the component parts of the stone. They use the term *coniunctio,* which simply means "union." Gerald Dorn, a leading German alchemist and disciple of Paracelsus, speaks a great deal of these stages of union. He not only outlines the nature of the three stages but speaks at length about the process within each. I find in Dorn's work an excellent model for understanding ally work and its practices. For the sake of simplicity, I will consider the way in which the three stages of union relate to ally work by equating one of the alchemical components, mercury, to the ally and the other, sulfur, to the partner.

In the first *coniunctio,* the interaction between sulfur and mercury has just begun. The goal of the alchemist is to combine these two in a union out of which emerges a new state of being. Dorn calls the first union, the mental union. Earlier, I mentioned the idea that the Stone possesses spirit, soul, and body and Dorn uses these three concepts to help explain the nature of the first union. The first level of union deals in particular with that between soul and spirit, which are first removed from the body. The first union therefore creates a bond between soul and spirit, but removed from any physical form. There are two reasons for this procedure: soul and spirit cannot unite while remaining in the body, and the extraction of both from the body remove them from the negative influences of the body. This, of course, had meaning in the alchemical context, but C. G. Jung discovered its relevance for psychology.

In Jung's process of individuation, by which a person achieves unique wholeness, uniting the unconscious and the conscious mind is a necessary part of the work. In Dorn's conception of attainment, *spirit* symbolizes the unconscious and *soul* consciousness. Thus, the extraction of both from the body in order to create a bond between them means that the conscious mind examines and relates to the products of the unconscious. It makes no attempt to embody what it discovers, so the contact between the two remains a purely mental state. Applying this idea to ally work, the soul would correspond to the human and the spirit to the ally. The body symbolizes the level of integration that the union has achieved. If the spirit and soul are united without being in a body, it means that the union consists of an interaction between ally and partner, but not in a permanent state. The more the body is developed the more the union has achieved a permanent state, meaning that the partner is continuously aware of the ally no matter what else is occurring.

The first step toward creating a permanent union with the ally occurs in the second *coniunctio*, in which spirit and soul are placed once more in a body. The body symbolizes a permanent container for the union, which means that the partner has created a life in which he or she is connected with the ally more or less all the time. This is difficult to achieve, but worth the effort, for it fills your life with the loving support of the ally and goes far to unite imaginal and ordinary reality.

In the third *coniunctio*, termed the *unus mundus* by Dorn, the ally and its partner explore imaginal space together and experience processes connecting them with other imaginal entities. At this stage, the two partners recognize a shared purpose and begin to carry it out in both imaginal and ordinary reality.

I have divided the practices into three sections, with each section corresponding to one of the three levels of union. The practices are designed to help create the particular level at which they are presented. Thus, the first set of practices are designed to bring about the first *coniunctio*, and so on. By organizing the practices in this fashion, I hope to provide a clear sense of their use in the overall goal of creating a union with the ally.

In conclusion, ally work consists of forming a relationship with the ally by paying attention to it, with the maximum benefit to both parties. Ally work therefore requires constant effort to improve your imaginal skills. The practices that follow are designed to guide you into a relationship with the ally as well as improve your ability to imagine.

CHAPTER 2

The Principles of Ally Work

Having established what ally work consists of, let's look at its main features in more detail. By describing the principles of ally work, I hope to reveal more facets of its nature and experience. At the same, time I hope to uncover some of the mysteries connected to this work and further relate it to the alchemical procedures.

Ally Work Consists of Attending to the Ally

The first principle of ally work is that it involves paying attention to the ally. I have already stated this, but want to examine what that means more closely. It is an interesting concept that the attention of a human being helps a divine being grow and transform. It is important to examine the question of why this happens. In fact, Dr. Jung struggled with this phenomenon and offered some interesting ideas. He discovered that attention has fascinating properties, of which he wrote in his study of alchemical symbolism:

> The attention given to the unconscious has the effect of incubation, a brooding over the slow fire needed in the initial stages of the work; hence the frequent use of the terms *decotio*, digestion, *putrefactio*, *solutio*. It is really as if attention warmed the unconscious and activated it, thereby breaking down the barriers that separate it from consciousness.[9]

Attention acts like fire in the alchemical process, stirring the dense substance into life and activity. Attention brings the unconscious to life, and it acts in the same manner with the ally. It is not so much that attention brings the ally to life, but that it quickens its growth and initiates processes of transformation. At the same time, attention forms the link that binds the ally to its partner. Attention is as essential to ally work as fire is to alchemy for it achieves several different goals.

In the first place, attention implies being with, so that if you attend to the ally, you *relate* to the ally. If one does not attend to the ally in this sense, there can be no relationship. This may seem so obvious as to need no mention, but the unfortunate fact is that many people do not realize how important spending time with the ally actually is. One of the direst results of the cultural repression of the imagination is the feeling that if we spend time imagining, we are wasting time. Our culture equates time with material worth, so everything in life appears to be more compelling and important than working with the ally or spending any time in the imaginal. Just as we begin to work with the ally, we remember that the laundry has to be done, or the bills need to be paid, or the phone answered, and so there is just no time to spend in imagining. There is, of course, a time for the mundane chores of life, but normally they may await our return from visiting the imaginal, for this visit takes no more than an hour. But as we ready ourselves for the inner exploration, the voices of the mundane arise in a choir, chanting their demand for immediate attention.

The most common report I hear from beginners is that, although they meant to, they haven't had time for a visit with the ally for a month or so. Yet they also are often surprised that they haven't dreamed of the ally or had some experience of it in that time. Imagine dating someone and failing to call them for a month because you were too busy. When you do get around to calling, what reception do you think you'll get? It is the same with the ally relationship. It requires attention and commitment. In this regard there are really no excuses for failing to make a certain amount of time available for this work. You either do or do not, and the degree to which you do is the measure of your commitment.

Another function of attention is to focus on a particular issue. For example, you might choose to focus your attention on eradicating a bad habit, learning about your unconscious responses to authority figures, or ways of connecting to the ally. Whatever you focus on receives a powerful impact from this attention. With such attention comes a responding movement within the imagination, as an imaginal figure responds, or you dream about the issue in question. In whatever form it occurs, there is a response to the attention you give to the imaginal that is noticeable and often impressive, and this is so important that I recommend to people doing imaginal work that they consciously choose what to attend to before staring the work. In particular, I call the focus the imaginal figure to which you will pay particular attention. In this book you shall mostly focus on the ally, but there are some practices in which you will focus on other figures as well. As a general rule, a focus concentrates attention on an imaginal figure with which you plan to dialogue and to work on achieving the intent of dialogue.

Coupled with the focus is what I call "intent," which is another function of attention. Intent forms an important part of ally work, for it establishes what you hope to achieve at a particular time. Having intent places your attention on an outcome that you find desirable or helpful. When I discuss each practice, I shall describe the intent and focus that accompanies it. Intent is not an attempt to control the experience, but to fix attention on a desired outcome. If, for example, I choose for my focus developing a deeper relationship to the ally, and my intent is to feel the ally more clearly, I must next allow the experience to unfold as it will, without forcing it into the direction I want. Knowing what your goal is allows the ally to respond to it. It might tell you that it cannot create the outcome you seek, or you are not ready, or it might help you obtain the goal. Whatever the response is, it is evoked by placing attention on the intent desired.

The esoteric tradition recognized the power of attention as well. In Kabbalah, in particular, there developed a concept of *kawanah*, or intention, which had to do with paying attention to the higher divine world while praying or performing ritual activity. Kabbalists recognized the importance of intention and attention and linked both to imagination. They believed that imagination was creative and theurgic; that is, imagination could impact God and cause changes in the divine realms. As Moshe Idel, a scholar of the Kabbalah, explains:

> According to this understanding, *kawanah* effects an elevation of human thought from the words of prayer to the sefirotic realm, apparently achieved without any intermediary mental operation or external factor. The intrinsic affinity of language to its sources in the divine realm enables human thought to ascend to the Sefirot and to act upon them.[10]

The Sefirot are the aspects of God. Through imagination and attention, then, the Kabbalist hoped to transform God and cause divine energy to descend into the world. Success or failure depended on the ability to attend to the words and to imagine that they were related to the divine world. In the same way, intention is a creative and transformative force that guides the imaginative process in a particular direction.

Attention is therefore a powerful tool that needs to be used consciously. By having a focus, I make clear to myself where I am placing my attention so that I make the maximal use of its effect. By having intent, I alert myself and my ally to the goal I wish us to accomplish together. Having such a goal with the ally strengthens our partnership by establishing what we hope to achieve together and, through the power of attention, intent makes it more likely that we will succeed.

I find that whenever I teach about intent, some individuals grow uneasy. They tell me they feel it is wrong for them to have a goal because that might interfere with what the ally wants. They feel that intention is somehow too ambitious and controlling, and could lead to inflation, a mistaken belief in one's power and grandeur. Others feel that the ally alone should decide what the goal should be, and they are prepared to surrender their will to the ally.

In some ways these individuals are correct in hesitating to have intent, for there is danger in inflation. Yet the interesting thing is that the ally usually follows its partner's intent and that, often, if there is no intent the ally does not work for anything in particular. It, too, has goals that it may impart to its partner, but the partner needs to provide the attention that makes the process work. That also means attention for a goal, so if there is no intent there is little progress. There is no need to fear inflation or usurping the ally's role if you remain in relationship, for the ally will tell you if there is any problem. The ally does not have to follow the intent and can choose not to, if it is inappropriate. It is therefore better to overreach than not to reach at all, for the ally will correct any error but cannot provide the will. Being an equal partner also means that you and the ally have the right to propose goals and to make any suggestions desirable.

In this partnership, the human partner provides attention and intention, and the ally creates results. If the ally does not approve of the intention, it does not cooperate, but if it does, it sets in motion processes by which the intent will be brought to fruition. Thus, each partner has an appropriate place in the relationship. For this partnership to work, however, the ally's partner must formulate questions and intentions that support the relationship. In this work, you will be walking a tightrope between being too humble or too arrogant.

Our society has a peculiar relationship to power. Our religious values emphasize humility and meekness, while our cultural values laud the rich and powerful. Psychology does not avoid this contradiction either, and Jung rejected ego domination and control while trying to make clear how important the ego is to the individuation process. He does not always succeed in his writing; the result is that some Jungians reject power in theory and seem plagued by it in practice. A healthy attitude toward power neither rejects it nor makes it bad, but allows you to accept and use it well. In ally work, the partner must accept his or her role and the need for power, while putting love and relationship to the ally as the first priority. As humans, we are not masters of the universe, but neither are we insignificant worms. We are partners with the divine in helping the universe grow and in bringing light into the darkened world.

There is no greater delight than working with an ally to achieve a worthwhile goal, whether it is interpreting a dream, answering a metaphysical question, transforming a complex, or changing our position in the world. To achieve these goals, we must dare ask the ally to help us accomplish them. We must also focus our attention on these goals with the intention of accomplishing our task. In my experience, people approaching ally work are not inflated, but are in fact too hesitant to ask for what they want and too content to wait and see what happens. Such an attitude guarantees that you will wait; often for a very long time.

Alchemical writings contain much insistence on cultivating humility and all the virtues. At the same time, however, the alchemists repeat often that the Philosopher's Stone is not found in nature. What they mean by this is that the Stone requires both alchemy and alchemist to come into existence. Without the alchemist, there can be no Philosopher's Stone. Moreover, as Jung first emphasized, the alchemist is convinced that he or she must redeem the universe and not wait for redemption to come to them. The alchemist must take an active role in order to effect this redemption which, once again, cannot occur without him or her. Salomon Trismosin wrote, in 1582:

Thus, this art possesses a wondrous thing, its beginnings rooted in nature that which nature could never give birth by itself; for nature by itself could never produce the thing through which the metals, imperfectly made by nature, can be born.[11]

Alchemy creates the Stone, which nature cannot produce, and heals the imperfect metals which is one of the many symbols for redemption.

It is important to keep in mind the alchemical symbolism about redemption and the generation of the Stone, for considering these symbols reminds us of the important role we each play in the enterprise. Alchemy, like other esoteric traditions such as the Kabbalah, knows the value of the human soul and mind. Recognizing this value does not invite inflation but the courage required to do what we must do. The first principle of ally work, then, is attention; focus and intent are ways to consciously work with this principle.

Dialoguing with the Ally

In order to relate with the ally, we must communicate with it. Such communication naturally occurs within the imaginal realm. There are many ways to imagine and so many ways to access the imaginal. You can dance, or move your body, paint, visualize images, or talk with the imaginal being. Of all the possible methods, I find dialogue the most useful for ally work. I generally recommend that dialogues be written rather than merely spoken, because writing grounds the experience in a way that is unique, and preserves the memory of what was said forever. Despite the feeling that you are having an unforgettable dialogue, it tends to vaporize the same way as dreams sometimes do. Writing insures that you do not lose what you have gained. At the same time, writing facilitates the experiences. People generally do better when they begin the practice with writing, rather than sitting and waiting for something to speak with them. Writing lends itself well to the type of exercises I shall present later. Though people sometimes feel more comfortable with other techniques for contacting the imaginal, there is much to be gained by writing dialogues that, in my view, cannot be had in any other way.

As I teach it, then, ally work consists in writing dialogues with the ally. Though at the later stages this method gives way to powerful, direct experiences, such experiences might never come without the writing practice preparing the way. Writing dialogues effectively draws the ally and its partner closer together, facilitates the exchange of information, and provides the much-needed attention for the ally. Even with the advantages writing presents, learning to dialogue is not easy and may take much practice. In my experience, everyone can learn to do it, given enough patience and effort. The opening exercises are designed to teach dialoging and later ones deepen skills needed for this practice.

One way to appreciate the value of the dialogue is to imagine forming a new relationship with a person whom you find interesting and attractive. Imagine forming a new relationship without being able to speak to the person. Think how hard it would be to get to know them and to learn what they liked and disliked and what their interests were. It would, of course, be difficult to do, and the same is true for the relationship to the ally. The ally is a living being with its own consciousness and personality, and the best way to get to know that being is to talk with it. It is remarkable how quickly the ally relationship develops and deepens when dialogues take place. Students who felt they could get nowhere discovered, after mastering the technique of the dialogue, how quickly the relationship transformed.

Given its great value, I believe that dialogue is a fundamental principle of ally work. It is of interest to note the role dialogue played in alchemy. We might not tend to think of alchemists engaging in dialogue since they are usually depicted as proto-chemists working before the retort and fire. Yet many of them knew the technique of dialogue and used it to good effect in their alchemical work. Ruland, who wrote a lexicon of alchemy, defined meditation as the "name of an internal talk of one person with another who is invisible, as in the invocation of the Deity, or communion with one's self, or with one's good angel." The "good angel," by the way, has much in common with the ally.

Jung also realized that the dialogue was an important method in alchemy and he connected it with attention. He comments that meditation implies that, "through a dialogue with God yet more spirit will be infused into the stone. . ."[12]

With the newly-added spirit, the Stone moves through its processes more quickly. Dialoguing focuses attention and at the same time brings into the process the power and energy of the entity with which you dialogue. In ally work, dialoguing with the ally brings the power of the ally into the process while guiding it through the placing of attention. Dialoguing was used in alchemy not only to acquire information but to activate and direct the energies the alchemist required to achieve the creation of the Stone. In the same way dialoguing leads, through relationship to the ally, toward the achievement of our goals.

Perceiving And Mirroring

This principle is more complex but of no less importance than the previous two. In the imaginal realm, perception has a different result than in the ordinary world. Imaginal perception is not only an act by which we see an object, it is also an act that transforms both the seer and the seen. Perhaps an analogy will help explain this. An artist first has an image of a painting she wishes to do. She holds that image in mind while she paints, and in the end her finished work looks like her first image. Now imagine that she is like Pygmalion and has the power to bring her picture to life. The picture began as an image and then moved into outer reality as a painting and, finally, came alive as a living being.

Perception is related to attention and it is through the act of seeing an imaginal entity that the entity becomes more real. The more I see the ally, the more real the ally becomes. The ally then presents itself to me in the way in which it wishes to be seen and, by my seeing it, it becomes more clearly what it first presented. There is a dynamic, active relationship that forms in the imaginal realm when a person perceives an ally or other imaginal figure. Since transformation is so large a part of ally work, it is very significant that transformation occurs through perception. Perception may be visual, but it may be auditory or take place through writing as well.

The ability of perception to effect the ally powerfully is a fact that I first observed in my own experience, but I later found that there were other traditions that noted this as well. Among the Sufi mystics, perception also has a great deal of power, and the Sufis, who were often alchemists, also noted the mirroring nature of the ally relationship. The Sufi Gnostics, or knowers of truth, developed doctrines similar to ally work. In some of their schools, they taught that a person could have direct perception of the angelic beings who run the universe, which has three major results. It connects the individual directly with the ruling forces of the universe and establishes, at least potentially, a relationship between them as well as transformation of each by the other. It allows for the possibility of attaining direct knowledge about the universe through dialogue and other interactions with these angels. Finally, these angelic beings not only teach and guide the individual, but by increasing the frequency and depth of contact with them, the Gnostic increases his or her own visionary capacities to the point that the imaginal world becomes more accessible to their sight. This opens up limitless possibility for increased gnosis as well as transformative experiences.

The Sufi Gnostics also taught that perceptual relationship is the hallmark of work with the angelic beings. One of their teachers informs students that they may first perceive their heavenly partner, or ally, as a dark light, but that is only due to their perceptual weakness (see, for example, Henry Corbin's discussion, "Heavenly Witness," in *The Man of Light in Iranian Sufism*). Soon they will see it as all forms of color, ending with a bright golden light. The more they see the ally the more able to see they become. With each act of perception, their organs of perceptions increase in power. I might paraphrase these ideas by saying that we begin the work with an undeveloped imagination, but the more we work with the ally, the more the imagination opens and reveals many dimensions of reality. At the same time that my perceptual skills increase, the ally too transforms, becoming more real and less ethereal. As we develop objective reality and the felt sense, the ally becomes more present and substantial, as if, through our increased perceptual ability, the ally takes on more substance. It is not clear if the ally's incarnating improves our imaginal skill or vice versa, but that is not important. What is important is that the relationship grows as perception does, and as the relationship grows so does perceptual skill.

Keeping in mind the Sufi notion of angels, we can say that dialogue with the ally—or what the Sufis call the Angel of one's Being, we are brought into relationship with the divine core of the universe. Dialoguing empowers our perception and perception enriches dialogue. The nature of this relationship is experiential and perceptual and never remains intellectual or theoretical. As our perception of the ally quickens, the ally appears more real.

Modern physics teaches that there is no separation between observer and observed. The act of observing alters the object observed. So, too, in ally work the act of observing the ally changes the ally and alters the relationship between the observer and the observed. As mentioned, the ally becomes more real. But what does it mean to say that the ally becomes more real? How can the ally become more real if it is already real?

To understand what I mean it is necessary to recall our map of reality. The upper world of pure spirit remains unknown to us. Spiritual beings such as the ally enter the middle, imaginal world in order to be perceived. By the same token, we enter the imaginal world in order to perceive them. However, the ally does not enter the imaginal world all at once. It is as if the image it creates for itself can only hold a certain amount of the ally's energy, so it remains relatively weak and indistinct. When a person enters the imaginal realm, he or she brings along a certain amount of skill or knowledge that facilitates perception of an imaginal figure. A person with more skill may perceive more clearly than someone who has less skill. As our skills increase, we can discern more of the imaginal space. In a similar way, the ally has a limited capacity to incarnate in the imaginal realm and only if that capacity increases does it become more apparent in every way. As ally work progresses therefore, the ally image becomes stronger and holds more of the energy of the ally so that the ally incarnates in the image. As a result, the image gains in power and distinctiveness. It seems to the partner that his or her ally has become more real. Just as it is our goal to increase our perceptual abilities, it is the ally's goal to bring more of its personality into the image it has forged. Ultimately, the image and the ally are one.

There is a parallel process in alchemy. Alchemists used color change to indicate a change in the quality of the Stone they were trying to create. The normal sequence was to begin with black, move to white, and then conclude with red. As each color appeared in the material, the alchemists presumed a change had occurred. They portray the change with many images, but the one that relates most clearly to the process under discussion has to do with the tripartite division of body, soul, and spirit. For our purposes it is not necessary to define each of these terms, but it is important to note the changes that occur in the Philosopher's Stone as each of these three is added to it.

In the black phase, all we have is a dead body, the residue of the previous material with which we start the alchemical process. This corresponds to the weak state of the ally's image at the beginning of the work. The alchemists know that the body is weak, but the black body at the same time is the most perfect body capable of transforming. As it transforms, it gains the ability to host a divine being. As the black turns to white, the alchemists imagine that they have added the spirit to the body, bringing it to life. As it moves into the red, they suppose they have added the soul, making the Stone a whole being consisting of body, soul, and spirit. One alchemist explains that the end result is that the "heavenly has assumed an earthly body, and that the earthly body has been reduced to a heavenly substance."[13] The same alchemist likens the process to the creation of Adam and Eve. He is by no means alone in ascribing the birth of a divine entity to the process. By the time that the heavenly assumes an earthly body, the ally has incarnated in the image and become powerful and real.

In terms of our previous discussion of imaginal experience, as the ally becomes more real it has a stronger felt sense and takes on more objective reality. Its partner notices the differences in the experience, as the objective presence of the ally has dramatically increased. It is through the attention and perception of the partner that the ally transforms in this way. Since it is through perception that the change occurs, I emphasize the perceptual nature of the relationship and the great power perception has at all stages of ally work.

Love

Above all else, this is a relationship of love. From the moment the ally presents itself, whether in dreams or in waking imaginal experience, it conveys its love and acceptance. Love is the predominant felt experience in ally work, and it deepens as the relationship does, growing with each new experience. I do not speak of a human love that has as its object another person with definable properties, but a love that extends toward a being that is never an object, for it is indefinable. You love the ally and are loved in turn, but you do not define the ally or the content of the love. It is as if you love by entering into the experience of love itself. When the ally is present, you are in love and in the experience of love, but what you love is difficult to say. Such concerns are of little import, but the point needs making that the relationship between human and ally should not be thought in terms of relationship between two people. It is a unique relationship that needs to be experienced on its own terms.

One of the unique features of this relationship is that it competes with no other relationship. One of the questions I am often asked is how will my love for the ally influence my primary relationship? People sometimes feel guilty that they love another besides their spouse, but this is of no concern to the ally. Since loving the ally is an experience of love itself, it only serves to increase our love for others. It neither competes nor is the ally jealous. In fact, the ally discourages the idea of living alone to have an exclusive relationship, and actively encourages other primary relationships. Since one of the ally's goals is the uniting of ordinary and imaginal worlds, it encourages your full participation in the affairs of everyday life.

Though people rarely think of alchemy in terms of love, the alchemists knew a deep love for the Philosopher's Stone and felt themselves loved in turn. One alchemist ecstatically celebrates the making of the Stone in terms of love:

> Now is the stone shaped, the elixir of life prepared, the lovechild or child of love born, the new birth completed, and the work made whole and perfect. O wonder of wonders![14]

Because of the deep love existing between the ally and its partner, the former never willingly brings harm to its partner. It protects and nourishes, though it can push hard if its partner neglects the work. We may trust it implicitly, counting on the love it bears. There is, however, one note of caution that must be sounded and this brings me to the fifth and last principle of ally work.

The Ally Is not Perfect

This is a very important principle to keep in mind when working with the ally. The supposition that spiritual beings, whether divinities or angels, are perfect, is ingrained in the psyche. Of course there are traditions such as alchemy and Kabbalah that take note of the imperfect state of the universe, but for the most part, religious traditions take for granted the perfection of deity. Students invariably project this perfection onto the ally, forgetting that ally work concerns itself with the ally's transformation. In other words, the ally presents itself in an imperfect condition to its partner, requiring transformative processes. Far from being perfect, it needs human help to develop.

At a practical level, this has important implications. I mentioned earlier that the process of ally work results in the ally becoming more real. As it gains this reality, it becomes stronger and capable of extraordinary feats. It gains in wisdom, as well. Of course, compared to the "ordinary" human, the ally is very powerful and wise, but compared to what it could be, the ally is tiny indeed. If you ask it to predict the future or to heal someone or something, and it agrees, it might fail or be wrong because it may lack the power to achieve the goal. It rarely gives wrong advice and is never wrong about what needs to happen in the process, but if you tax it with goals requiring power, it might not succeed. The best course of action is to relate to the ally as a source of wisdom and guidance, but not as a being capable of accomplishing any goal. Sometimes because of its love for its human partner, the ally might try to heal or perform nonordinary events, but this is no guarantee of success. If the ally does make a mistake or fail at a task, the partner frequently feels betrayed, as if the ally purposely lied. That is why it is crucial to keep in mind that the ally is not omnipotent. You should look forward to growing with the ally in love and wisdom, knowing that there will come a time for extraordinary experiences. Yet the goal is not the extraordinary but the relationship itself. If the ally tells its partner something that turns out to be false, the partner should ask the ally what went wrong rather than assume it was all a trick. Usually it becomes apparent that the request was misguided or the ally simply could not perform it. If you truly love the ally, you will accept its shortcomings and seek the path of mutual growth.

In this chapter I provided enough theory to make the exercises to come understandable and to give you a sense of what constitutes ally work. Much of what I have explained will only make sense once you begin the work, so it is time now to proceed to the first set of practices.

PART II

First Coniunctio
Beginning Practices

CHAPTER 3

The Journey Commences

Beginning practices are for individuals who have never done ally work as well as those who have an ally but have not yet established a stable union with it. Those who are still working to create a sense of permanent connection with the ally, as well as those who have never had an ally, will benefit from these exercises. Individuals who already have an ally but feel they need help in deepening the relationship with it will benefit as much as those who do not yet have an ally.

Before discussing the first practice, there are four rules of thumb the beginner should be aware of. Since attention has the power to increase the growth of an imaginal figure, *the first rule of thumb is pay attention to only what you wish to grow*. It is rarely a good idea to pay attention to a hostile or negative figure. If you hear a very critical voice, for example, you should not debate with this voice or try to convince it that it is wrong. Paying attention to it in this way actually strengthens the critical voice and may even result in your being caught by it; that is, you come to believe that it is speaking truth. Rather than speaking directly to a negative voice, you should talk to the ally *about* the negative voice. If the ally thinks it is worth integrating this voice then you can work directly with it. Using the ally instead of a negative inner figure provides protection and yet will allow consideration to be given to your darker side if that becomes necessary.

The second rule of thumb is to respect your work. When you write down your ally work, you are recording the products of your soul and the words of your beloved companion. It therefore makes sense to treat such a text as worthy of respect and careful consideration. You may discover that the more you review your work, the more you learn. But what is the usual attitude toward such work? It is usual for people to be critical and judge the work harshly. I have heard people criticize their work from many perspectives. They find it dull, without merit, commonplace, not as exciting as other people's work or, if they do find it interesting, they are sure it is all made up and unreal. Many times I have witnessed students' profound and moving experiences only to see them come to me later and tell me they thought it was all nonsense after all.

There are many reasons that this critical voice appears and it plagues creative writers and painters as well as those doing ally work. The destructive power of this inner critic is not to be underestimated. Whatever its source, the only way to deal with it is to ignore it as much as possible. This is not always easy, because the voice can be very convincing in its attacks.

The attitude you should try to instill is that of respect for your work. It is a good idea to mark the beginning and end of your work time with a ritual of some sort, reminding yourself that you are engaging in spiritual work; sacred work that should be protected from all criticism. This does not mean you do not think carefully about what you have written or that you accept it without reflection. In fact, you should reflect upon it a great deal. You can make notes, write down questions, and challenge the ally about your exchange. But this is very different from discounting or denigrating the work. Even if you disagree with what the ally has said, you need to consider it carefully and as deserving of regard. You will find as you do this work that you can challenge the ally without harming your relationship to it, but the critical voice does injure the relationship. It can even end the relationship by creating mistrust and a tendency to ignore the work. You should protect yourself as much as possible by ignoring the critic and respecting the work.

The third rule is to approach the work with a spirit of creative play. While it is important to respect the work, it is just as important to have fun doing it. The ally is very playful and joyful, and dialoguing with it should also be enjoyable. After doing it for a while, you will begin to look forward to it. However, at the beginning of the work, people put pressure on themselves to perform and sometimes expect miraculous visitations or great insights. Not every dialogue brings revelations, but they are all equally important in creating the relationship with the ally. If you expect too much or try too hard, very little occurs. As I shall soon make clear, visiting the imaginal realm requires spontaneity and a willingness to imagine, and imagining is playing. If you are willing to play, the possibilities are endless. If you wonder what creative play is like, recall how you played as a child and how your toys and dolls were filled with life. This by no means implies that your dialogues never concern difficult and painful topics, or that they can't be difficult to experience because of their intensity and content. It is rather that your attitude should be one of playful openness even when there are difficult problems to address.

While dialoguing, it is essential to discard as completely as possible negative attitudes toward the imagination. If you still suppose that imagination is unreal or false, you will struggle with the work. To enter fully into ally work requires the ability to let go and play with freedom, spontaneity, and trust.

The fourth axiom is related to the last one: You need to remember and integrate the experience. Dialogues can be very powerful, but like dreams, they are easily forgotten. That is one reason I recommend writing down your dialogues for, when you are done, you have a record of the work as it unfolded. Having that record allows you to read and reread what you have written, giving you the opportunity to reflect on the experience and, as you read, to actually re-experience it as well. At the same time, you are reminded of what has been learned and perhaps what has not yet been.

I have found myself reading experiences I had twenty years ago and benefiting from them again. It is always amazing to me how much I have forgotten and yet how consistent the experiences have been over the years. I was also able to determine whether I had made the experience part of my life, for that is the most important result of the work. Bringing what you have gained into your life is called integration.

Integration is the process by which you make real what you have learned and weave it into your attitude and behavior. To give a simple example, if the ally asks you to talk with it several times a week, and a few weeks later you are still talking with it every day or two, we can say that you have integrated the message. On the other hand, if at the end of a few weeks you have forgotten all about the ally, then we can say you have failed to integrate it. It is important to integrate the ally's messages for it helps to bring the imaginal world into daily life. Integration brings the world of ordinary reality closer to the imaginal realm and allows you, in time, to experience the imaginal in the midst of the ordinary. An important aspect of ally work is bringing your everyday world into harmony with the imaginal.

The practices presented in this chapter cover the stage denoted in alchemy as the first *coniunctio*. The first union consists of the partner being aware of the ally and trying to relate with it as much as possible. At this point, the partner's awareness of the ally is not consistent and is intermittent. The goal of the first level, however, is not to create a permanent state. It is a process involving partner and ally in mutual exploration. The first level requires a willingness to introvert and turn the attention within to the ally.

Achieving a permanent state takes a great deal of work and involves a transformation of both ally and partner. In the beginning, or first level of union, permanence is not our goal. The goal of the first union is to learn to relate with the ally; to take it seriously and make every effort you can to be in contact. In the beginning of the first stage, the partner must first meet and get to know the ally. The first set of practices, therefore, aims at introducing you to the ally and establishing the beginning of the first union.

CHAPTER 4

Practice 1: Imaginal Play

The first practice is very basic, and yet essential for all further work. It is designed to introduce you to the imaginal by encouraging you to imagine freely and playfully. At the same time, it introduces you to the ally's voice, which you must get to know well. Additionally, this practice is the first step toward beginning a dialogue with the ally and helps build the skills required for such dialogues. Finally, this practice introduces you to one of the most important ideas in ally work: lending your mind to the ally.

Carl Jung introduced the profound idea of lending one's mind in his discussion of active imagination. The ally communicates by entering the psyche and creating images and words. It is as if the ally communicates by thinking with your mind; it forms thoughts and words in response to your thoughts and words. Eventually you find yourself in the position of the alchemical *rebis*; that is, there are two heads in one body. In time there are two centers of consciousness that speak with each other and exist together in one psyche. However, at the beginning it is not easy for the ally to communicate in this way. We need to cooperate with it to make this process easier. This you accomplish by loaning your mind to the ally.

Lending your mind to the ally consists of opening yourself to the possibility of hearing it within your mind or speaking with your voice. It is possible, through the imagination, to focus on the voice of the ally within. In this first practice, we work on doing just that.

This practice, like all the rest, takes a minimum of 30 minutes. It is important you find a quiet place where you will not be disturbed during the practice. As mentioned earlier, it is best to mark this time as sacred and to refuse to be distracted by any intrusion. These exercises are important not only for what you may accomplish through them but also for establishing a commitment to the ally relationship. The greatest obstacle to the work takes the form of distractions. No sooner do you begin the dialogue than a host of thoughts crops up, diverting your attention from the work at hand. Remember that behind every distraction lies a resistance to the work, and the simple act of staying focused on the ally is powerful in reducing the power of resistance and strengthening your bonds with the ally. Devoting an unbroken period of time to the ally is a mark of respect and a way of paying attention, which is just what the ally requires. In ally groups, one of us always kept time to let others know when to stop. When doing this work alone, you might want to set up an alarm so you know when time is up without having to constantly check the clock. Don't use a loud or annoying alarm but one that gently announces the end of the session. Resisting the temptation to follow a distracting thought is proof of your commitment to the ally. I recall hearing a teacher of mine berate a student who stopped her active imagination because her legs hurt. He scolded her for giving in to the resistance and reminded her that the more tension one feels in an active imagination, the more powerful the experience can be. Give the ally thirty minutes—which is not much time really—but a longer time may be necessary if you are beset by distractions. Make your commitment, keep it, and the work will progress.

The alchemists recognized this need for uninterrupted effort and strong commitment in their work as well. As Basil Valentine wrote about his powerful substance of antinomy, to speak truly of it "requires profound Meditations, a mind largely unfolding it self, and knowledge of its manifold *Preparation*, and of the true *Soul* of it . . . the more diligently any Man seeks, the more he finds . . . Yet the Life of no one Man is sufficient for him to learn all the mysteries thereof."[15] The work must be done patiently, with great dedication and persistence, and yet the more you prevail, the more you experience. Nicholas Flammel assures us that he labored for over three years, "during which time I did nothing but study and labor," and finally was rewarded with the discovery of the Stone.[16] The other alchemists write in much the same fashion, insisting that without persistence and hard work, the Stone is never found.

I have always been struck by the impatience and unconscious arrogance of some who try to do this work. After a few weeks of effort, these people get annoyed if the ally does not appear with lightning and thunder, and give up the work in disgust after a few months when their expectations are not met. This is the work of many years but time is of less importance than effort. If you find the inner resources with which you can stay the course and work every day toward the creation of this relationship, you will never know disappointment. The work depends, above all else, on this commitment, and you can show it most powerfully by sticking to the task for whatever duration you have set for yourself. I recommend you devote at least 30 minutes to a practice, for it usually takes this long to relax and concentrate on the writing.

Having chosen when to work, you must next choose where. Finding the right spot is as important as making the time. Ideally, you can find one place in your home where you can do ally work. If possible do nothing else in that space but ally work. The more you work in one place the better, for, in time, the room takes on the qualities of your work. Using the same space encourages dialogues and facilitates becoming centered for the work. I have friends who drink coffee from one cup and one cup alone, and they never drink anything else out of that cup. They swear that the coffee tastes better, for the cup comes to taste like coffee. It is the same with your room; in time it comes to "taste" like the ally.

If you cannot devote one room to this work, find as quiet a place as you can as far away from telephones or other distractions as possible. It should be comfortable and perhaps have a desk or some place where you may write. Unlike other practices, it is not necessary to sit in a meditative posture; rather, you should be comfortable and may even recline on a couch or sit in a reclining chair. If you are so relaxed that you fall asleep, so much the better. Having rested, you can return to the practice with renewed vigor. Don't simply get up, but take a little more time to write.

Next you must decide how you will write the dialogue. Will you use a computer, or pen and paper? Do you write as you dialogue, or wait until you are finished to write it all down? These are matters of personal preference; mine is to write as I dialogue because I find it too easy to forget what has been said if I wait. I also prefer a nice fountain pen to a computer, for the pen feels special to me and even has a sacred quality. When I take the pen in hand, I know I am entering sacred space. However, others prefer the speed with which they can write on the computer and they feel that they keep up with the thoughts going on in their heads more easily this way. Your choice should be based on what works for you in creating a good atmosphere while helping you remember what occurred. If you choose to write longhand, it is a good idea to buy a nice journal in which to keep a record of your experiences.

Having prepared yourself in the above ways, you are ready to begin the process of encountering the ally.

To begin the first practice, then, find a time you can be alone, a space that is quiet and comfortable and bring your writing implements with you.

It is also important to know the intent and focus of every practice before you begin. For this practice the intent, or goal, is to learn to play with the inner voice and your focus will be listening to that inner voice. This practice is the simplest kind for it neither seeks to dialogue with the ally as yet, nor does it seek any particular figure to work with. Its purpose is to familiarize you with writing and with hearing the inner voice.

We live in the "real" world most of the time, and rarely shift our attention to the imaginal world. If we did, we would discover a world that was always present and always active. Whether we are aware of it or not, our imagination is always at work. In performing this practice, you try to become aware of this activity and to listen in, as it were, to overhear what is being said. However, this is not a question of sitting passively and waiting, but rather of actively engaging in writing to stimulate dialogue and imagery. The ultimate purpose of this practice is to teach us how to engage the imaginal and capture some of its products on paper.

As you might imagine, there are a number of ways you might contact the inner voice. Throughout this book, you will experiment with a number of them. Our approach for this practice is that of creative play.

Since you are not attempting to contact any particular figure, ask a particular question, or even establish dialogue, the procedure is simple. However, this is a good time to discuss the method of writing imaginal work in general and to lay down the method you can use in attempting all of these practices.

Stages of Active Imagination

In another book I outlined the major stages of active imagination,[17] and the interested reader may look there for a full discussion. For our purposes I will mention these steps as they relate to ally work.

1. *Get centered.* It is important that you feel connected to yourself before attempting to do imaginal work. You can begin by doing some physical exercises, deep breathing, or meditation practice, but the first step is to get centered and to calm the mind. If you have never done any meditation and do not know how to center, you might try counting breaths, or listening to the rhythm of your breathing, or the beat of your heart. Or you can simply close your eyes and allow your mind to drift. After a few minutes, you should start to feel more relaxed and in your body. You are now in a position to consider the focus and intent of the exercise.

2. *State your intent and focus.* Write down, on the top of your paper, the intent and focus of the practice. All through the practice you can look at the top of the

page to remind yourself of the goal of the practice and to refocus your thoughts.

3. *Focus your attention.* Next, put your attention on the focus. Usually the focus will be the ally and you will concentrate on the image or name of the ally. Focusing can mean different things to different people. I focus on the feeling of the ally, but you might focus on an image you have for it or the sound of its voice or repeating its name. For this practice, you need only focus on the writing itself since you are not connecting to any particular image.

4. *Wait quietly and then when you feel ready, begin writing.* Your attempt in this exercise is to engage in creative play. You are to focus on the writing with the intent of hearing your inner voice and expressing it in writing. Do not ask a specific question or address a specific figure—just begin writing. Write whatever comes to you to write and keep writing for the whole time without censoring or controlling. There is no right way to do this and no goal to achieve—just play with writing and words. However, you do not want to write from your ego, but from the inner voice, so *do not write as if you were crafting a paper or a story.* Keep writing with as little reflection as possible.

I have noticed what I call "waves of writing" when doing these practices. You might start out with a roar and write for 5 or 10 minutes without pause, but gradually you'll run dry, and the writing comes to a halt. As you write, it is as if you are riding a wave of energy that starts high but gradually diminishes, setting you back down, with no more to write. When this occurs, take a deep breath and start the process over again. Center and wait until you feel like writing and begin again. You may experience two or three of these waves in a half hour.

At the conclusion of the half hour, stop writing. Close your eyes once more and center. When you feel relaxed, open your eyes and read, uncritically, what you have written. Do not evaluate style or quality of the writing, but read what you have written with an open mind. Ask yourself what you find interesting in the material. Is there anything that surprises you or gets your attention? What do you find most interesting? Is there a feeling that you notice when you read? Pay close attention to the things that interest you and ask yourself what they might mean to you. Since the intent was to give your inner voice a chance to express itself, ask yourself if you believe that you made contact with your inner voice? If so, what are the qualities of this voice that interest you?

There are several obstacles you must overcome in order to do ally work. The first and most damaging is the inner critic. Specifically in this practice, the critic is liable to make you feel that you cannot write anything and that you have no imagination. If you *are* able to write, the critic will inform you that you have written meaningless nonsense. Remember, respect your work and defeat the critic simply by honoring what you have written. If you have trouble writing, relax and remind yourself that the purpose of the exercise is to play. You perform this practice simply by writing.

Since the intent of this practice is to give your inner voice a chance to express itself, determine whether it did. Use as criteria the questions: Was anything new given to me? Did anything I wrote spark my imagination and interest? If you answer "yes," then you may conclude that your inner voice communicated with you. Do not expect revelations or major insights at this point. Repeat this practice several times until you feel comfortable writing and playing with the inner voice. It may take several months, but don't be impatient to move on, even if it takes longer to become comfortable with the practice. When you are satisfied with your progress move on to Practice 2.

PRACTICE 1 REVIEW

Find a *time* to be alone and undisturbed. Find a quiet *place* to practice and bring your writing implements. Sit quietly for a few moments, and then write your intent, "Contacting my inner voice," on the top of the page.

Intent and Focus

The intent is to allow your inner voice to express itself. Focus on whatever comes into your mind.

Activity

Write without thought or criticism and with as much freedom and spontaneity as possible.

Obstacles

Beware of the inner critic and any self-doubt it generates.

Outcome

Ask yourself what you learned that was new or that sparked your interest.

CHAPTER 5

Practice 2: The Wisdom of Pretending

Simply by playing with your inner voice, you took the first step toward the first union. You will experience the first union when you have discovered the reality of the other and realized that you cannot live as if alone any longer. You have to consider the advice and needs of the other and be willing to enter into relationship with it whenever possible. So far, you have discovered the existence of the inner voice with which you can play whenever you like. You take a further step toward relationship in this exercise by attempting to contact an inner figure. You will not contact the ally yet, but use this practice to develop skills through which you can contact the ally in a future exercise. The specific skill you will focus on is that of lending your mind to an inner figure.

If you have ever observed children at play, either alone or with friends, you will have noticed how often they pretend. They play certain roles or talk with invisible friends, and find it easy to make up games and stories. The ability to pretend is connected with creative play and constitutes an important way to enter the imaginal. We all still retain the ability to pretend even though, as adults, we neglect this skill almost entirely. Creative writers often pretend to be the characters in their stories in order to gain insight into their nature and behavior. But pretending is not only a good way to enter the imaginal, it is a great way to lend our minds to an imaginal figure.

When you pretend to be an imaginal figure, especially if you can really put yourself into the practice, you can actually experience the consciousness of this figure. This is certainly only a beginning in the effort to experience an imaginal figure, but it is often profound in its own right. As you pretend to be a figure, that figure often comes alive in your imagining. It is hard at this point to know what we are "pretending" and what is coming to us from the other. In this way, what starts out as pretence becomes compellingly real.

When I ask participants at workshops to pretend to be a figure, they often raise objections. Some feel that this is not a real dialogue, since they are making it up, while others feel foolish and inhibited. Pretending, however, is imagining, and it is important to learn that imagining is an active and not a passive endeavor. To imagine does not mean that you sit with eyes closed in deep meditation waiting for something to happen. Imagining is creating through the use of a part of our soul not often used. To be active is not the same as to be controlling, nor does it mean we can produce anything we like. Rather, imagining is an act of perception in which we reach out to perceive something that is already there. By pretending, we reach out mentally to a consciousness not our own, even though it may feel familiar and almost like our own consciousness. By pretending, we unite some part of ourselves with something not ourselves.

This is more easily experienced than explained. As you imagine what the other figure says, it quickly becomes apparent that you are not just constructing the words, but experiencing them as coming to you from someplace within. Soon the words start to flow with such rapidity that you do not feel you are constructing them at all, but hearing them as they emerge.

Pretending in ally work means that you imagine that you are the imaginal figure you wish to dialogue with and you write for the voice of the other. In other words, when doing a dialogue, you will first write for your own voice, representing your position and perspective. You might, for example, say hello to the imaginal figure and ask why he appeared in a dream from the other night. Then you must change perspective and pretend to be the other figure who will answer. Imagine you are the imaginal figure and write down what you would say as that figure. When done with the response of the other, assume your own position once more and write what you wish to say. You switch back and forth between writing for yourself and writing for the imaginal figure. Of course you should try not to think too much, but give the imaginal figure as much spontaneous expression as possible. As you move back and forth between positions, you can feel a real shift in consciousness and quickly enough it is possible to feel the difference between yourself and the other. The more you pretend to be the other, the greater the chance that the thoughts of the other will reach you and communicate itself in the writing.

Preparing for this practice is exactly the same as the previous one. You must find a quiet space and a time in which you will not be disturbed for at least 30 minutes.

The intent of this practice is to make contact and dialogue with an imaginal figure, not the ally, by pretending to be that imaginal figure and to write for it. You may choose any figure you wish, but it is a good idea to start with one you may have dreamed about. The only guideline for choosing is that the figure should be one that you find interesting and would like to meet and talk with. Keep in mind that axiom of attending to that which you wish to grow and do not choose a figure you do not wish to empower.

Keeping this goal in mind, focus your attention first on yourself and then on the inner figure you are pretending to be. Focus your mind on that figure and imagine what it looks like, what it talks like, and what it might wish to say to you. Your imagination should be locked on this figure until you finish writing for it, and then attend to yourself again. Switch your attention back and forth until you are done.

Having chosen an inner figure to dialogue with, write its name on the top of the page. If you do not know its name, write down a brief description of the figure so you remember later who it was. Then write down your initial greetings to the figure. Imagine next what that figure is like and pretend you are it. Put yourself in its place as much as you can, then begin writing as if you were the inner figure speaking to you. Then make your response and return to pretending to be the figure. Switch back and forth in this way until you are done with the dialogue.

The inner critic is an obstacle in all of these exercises and there is nothing new to say about it. You might feel foolish pretending to be an imaginal figure, but imagine you are playing as a child does and put aside your pride. The more you can get into the character, the more fun and success you will have.

Another obstacle that may arise is confusion about who is thinking what. You might forget you are pretending and start thinking as the inner figure does for your part of the dialogue, or you might override the inner figure by just being yourself when writing for it. The best way to avoid such confusion is to have a ritual barrier between the figures in the dialogue. For example, after you finishing writing for yourself you might take 10 deep breaths, or close your eyes for 1 minute, then start pretending to be the inner figure. Likewise, when you finish writing for the inner figure, count 10 breaths or close your eyes for 1 minute before starting to write for yourself. Taking some time out in this way allows you to recenter and remind yourself of where you are in the process before continuing.

When done writing, take a few minutes to center and relax. Now read what you have written, pay attention to what is most interesting to you in the dialogue, and make some notes about what attracts your attention or what you have learned or observed. Finally, ask yourself whether you feel that you dialogued with the inner figure. Did you make good contact? What was the feeling of the inner figure like? Again, make some notes so you remember the experience later. If you decide you did make contact with the figure, you are ready to move on to the next practice. If not, please repeat it and try again.

This is a good practice to come back to when you wish to experience a new figure that might have appeared in a dream or in another imaginal experience. You can also use it to deepen your awareness of figures you already know. If you perform this practice enough, you will discover that when starting to pretend, you slide almost immediately into the consciousness of the other. You will also find it easier to let an inner figure communicate with you. In one sense, every active imagination is a game of pretend, but, as always with the imaginal, the pretence is very real.

Practice 2 Review

Find a time to be alone and a place where you will not be disturbed. Gather your writing tools, sit quietly for a few moments, and, having decided which imaginal figure you wish to connect with, write its name or description on the top of the page.

Intent and Focus

Your intent is to meet a specific inner figure of your choice. Focus your attention on your self as you begin, then shift to pretending to be the inner figure. Write as if you were the imaginal figure.

Activity

Write for 30 minutes, writing for both your self and the inner figure. Focus as much as possible on the mind of the inner figure and imagine that you are that figure as you write. If you cannot tell whose voice you are using, stop and center again. Begin to write first with your own voice and then shift to the voice of the other.

Obstacles

As always, the inner critic will attack your work. Remember to respect what you have written and ignore the critic as much as possible.

You may feel foolish about "making up" the voice of the other but remember, this is imaginative play: enjoy yourself.

You may forget which voice you are writing or you may confuse the two voices. Take your time and establish a ritual of short duration to mark the change of voices.

Conclusion

Reflect on what you have written. Consider the material that strikes you as the most interesting. Formulate any questions or comments that occur to you.

Ask yourself if you feel you made contact with the figure. If you believe you have, move on to Practice three. Otherwise, repeat this practice either with the same or a new figure. Repeat this practice when you wish to make contact with another imaginal figure.

CHAPTER 6

Practice 3: Getting Help from the Imaginal

In this practice, you will make several additions to your existing practice in order to deepen your experience of the imaginal figure. This is not easy and you need to be patient for it may take several times to accomplish. You will now have a specific intent coupled with a clear focus and will work toward establishing a dialogue with an imaginal figure. You will also learn a third way of working with the inner voice. With this practice, your deepening connection with an imaginal figure helps to prepare you to move into ally work.

For your intent, think of a question or issue that is currently of interest to you. For example, you might currently be working with a marriage problem or a exploring a new way of being, or have had questions concerning your life. Pick anything that is of real significance; formulate a question concerning it, and write that question on top of the page. Your intent is to answer this question. Keep your attention on this question and finding an answer for it throughout the practice. If your attention wanders, firmly but gently bring it back to the question. You may not find an answer in one sitting, but keep dialoguing until the time is up, or until you feel you have received the answer.

As for the focus, you may choose any imaginal figure with whom you wish to discuss this question. It may be the same figure from the last exercise or one that appears very wise. It should be a figure that you trust. If you have dreamed about this question or the issue to which it relates, you might choose a figure that appeared in the dream. Once you decide on the figure you will contact, write its name below the question.

You now have a specific goal, which is to answer your question. In this practice, therefore, you will know when you are finished for you will have reached your goal. Do not change questions or give up until you have answered this question, even if it takes weeks of practice. In order to do imaginal work well, you must have the patience to take one task at a time and work with it until it is accomplished. Jumping from one question to another or from one figure to another without feeling that anything has been accomplished is counterproductive. As in any great endeavor, you must take one step at a time.

The alchemists well knew the dangers of moving too quickly or jumping ahead of the process. They warn constantly to avoid this dangerous practice. Alchemy consists of a series of steps and stages, each of which is difficult to accomplish. We must be focused on the step that faces us and not be distracted by any other issue or question. One alchemist, in speaking of his dreams about the work, describes how the god Pan urged him not to give up at a difficult point, but to persevere:

> However hard or high a goal may be,
> However far the consummation seems
> To which your spirit ardently aspires,
> If artistry and intellect are joined
> With gentle, sacred, pious patience—then
> A worthy soul achieves his every wish,
> And reaps the fruits of his desired intent,
> Grown rich in virtues, joyful and content.[18]

The great advantage of having a specific intent and focus lies in the ability of attention to stimulate the imaginal world. Focusing the attention on one clear question helps direct the answer. It is also less easy to become confused about the dialogue and where it needs to go, for you steer it repeatedly in the direction set by the intent. The disadvantage is that getting a satisfactory answer takes time. Patience is essential in imaginal work, and it produces great rewards, just as it does in alchemy.

You now have a goal and a figure with which to work. Now we shall explore a new method of interacting with the imaginal figure and creating a dialogue. In the previous practice you pretended to be the imaginal figure and spoke in your voice and in its; in this one, you will speak in your voice, but *hear* the voice of the other. Learning to hear the voice of the imaginal figure takes practice. The best approach is to empty your mind as completely as possible and put all of your attention on the inner figure. Imagine it in as much detail as possible while waiting for it to respond in some way. Beginners make the common mistake of expecting to hear a voice speaking as they would a human voice, but such hearing occurs rarely. Remember that your goal is to lend your mind to the figure. The reason this is so important is that the figure communicates through thought, rather than through spoken word. Instead of hearing a voice *per se* you are more likely to find yourself thinking and if you are not observant you will allow that thought to pass through and be replaced by other thoughts. If you attend to the thought, however, you generally notice that it feels as if it were not coming from your mind but from the figure. It requires focus and concentrated attention to notice this when first learning, but after a while it is easy to spot the thoughts coming from the imaginal being.

Sometimes the figures communicate not in thoughts but in feelings, impulses, or body sensations. You must pay attention to these as well as actual thoughts in your mind, for they also form the vocabulary of the imaginal figure. When paying attention to the response of the imaginal figure, then, you need to observe anything that happens that does not seem to belong to your consciousness. If you ask a question and your leg itches, focus on that sensation. Keep your attention on that sensation or the emotion that arises until a thought process is triggered by it. Since you are most interested in a dialogue process, the sensation or emotion needs to move into a thought process through which the other expresses itself to you. Whatever the initial response to your question is, focus on it until thoughts arise from the other.

To begin, then, you focus on the inner figure by imagining it in detail, but when thoughts begin to arise in your mind, emotions occur spontaneously, or any of the possible reactions take place, you shift your focus to these. As thoughts appear in your mind, write them down and keep writing as long as the train of thought continues. As with free writing, you will probably experience a wave of thinking and writing that exhausts itself before another arises. A good practice is to allow the thought process to continue until it ceases on its own. At that point, having finished writing down the thoughts, relax and then respond to what you have heard.

The difficult part is differentiating your thoughts from those coming from the figure. Pay close attention to what is happening in your mind, for when your thoughts take an unusual direction or feel different than they do normally, assume these are coming from the other. If you are unsure, ask the imaginal being if that thought came from it. If you are still in doubt, assume that the thoughts did in fact come from the other and write them down. If you are wrong, you will discover this eventually and it is better to make a mistake by recording your own thoughts rather than missing the communication of the other. Because communication occurs within the thought process, people can become confused. This is the reason so many people feel that they "made-up" their dialogue. You will learn in time that each inner figure has a certain feel to it that makes it easier to recognize. You will also discover that the figure thinks things that you normally do not or cannot. Dr. Jung discovered that his ally, Philemon, "represented a force which was not myself. In my fantasies I held conversations with him, and he said things which I had not consciously thought. For I observed clearly that it was he who spoke, not I."[19] Philemon goes on to explain the mystery of thoughts to Jung:

> He said I treated thoughts as if I generated them myself, but in his view thoughts were like animals in the forest, or people in a room, or birds in the air, and added, "If you should see people in a room, you would not think that you had made those people, or that you were responsible for them." . . . Through him the distinction was clarified between myself and the object of my thought.[20]

In this remarkable passage, which incidentally is a good example of what one can learn from an ally, Philemon taught Jung that the thoughts arising in a person's mind do not necessarily belong to the conscious personality. They may in fact derive from an imaginal figure. These figures think within your mind when you are dialoguing, and, very likely, at other times as well. If you put away the prejudice that everything in the mind is under your control or derives from your will, you can practice differentiating your thoughts and determining their origins. If you can determine their origins, you can examine their meaning, instead of naively believing they are your thoughts and are to be taken at face value. For example, you might realize that you have been inundated with the thoughts of the inner critic and that you should not trust these thoughts. The idea that imaginal beings think within our minds is one that deserves far more attention than it has so far received.

In this practice, then, you try to isolate the thoughts coming from the figure, and write those down as the voice of the other. You then respond to these thoughts in an appropriate way, write down your voice, sit quietly until thoughts enter your mind once more, and then record these. The more you practice this procedure, the better, for it will serve well in all future practices.

There is one hint to keep in mind while attending to thoughts. One of the main ingredients of imaginal experience is the felt sense, and thoughts generated by imaginal figures typically have a different *feel* than those coming from your own mind. In fact, each figure has its own feeling which, after practice, you can learn to recognize. This helps a great deal in identifying the source of the thoughts. The inner critic, for example, always feels a certain way and makes us feel a certain way. It has a sharp, judgmental ,and harsh feel and it makes us feel badly about who we are or what we have done. As you pay attention to the thoughts in your mind, observe closely any felt sense they might possess, and keep track of which feeling corresponds to which thoughts.

In this practice you write for two voices: your own and that of the imaginal figure. Since you have a specific question in mind, you begin the dialogue by presenting this question to the other and then you wait for its response. It is important to get the dialogue started and to keep it moving. For example, if you have posed your question but have not noticed any thoughts emerging from the imaginal figure, you may pretend to be that figure and start writing. As you do, though, keep your attention on your thoughts and observe any train of thought that arises from the other. In this way you can use pretending to jump-start the dialogue and switch over to the new method when possible. This is preferable to waiting too long and getting discouraged. Part of the goal should be to maintain the dialogue for the full 30 minutes and use whatever tools you may to achieve this goal.

When the time has expired, relax for a few moments and read what you have written. Was your question answered? Did the answer satisfy you? If yes, why and if no, why not? If your question was not answered, did you nevertheless feel that you made contact with the imaginal being? If you do not feel you received an answer, keep working on this question until it is answered. Start the next dialogue exactly where you left off this one. It may take days or even weeks to receive a good answer and it is important to keep working on it and not switch to another topic. When you feel you have received an answer, move on to the next practice. You will observe that monitoring your thoughts will be part of most future practices so it is a good idea to do this practice many times.

PRACTICE 3 REVIEW

Find the time and place to do the practice. Choose a question you would like answered and write this down on the top of your page. Next, decide which imaginal figure you will dialogue with and write this down as well.

Intent and Focus

Your intent is to receive an answer to a question of your choice by establishing and maintaining a dialogue with the imaginal figure of your choice. Your focus is on the imaginal figure and any messages it gives to you. Imagine this figure in the greatest detail and pay attention to any thought or feeling deriving from the figure.

Activity

Write for two voices. First, write for your own voice and then wait, focusing on the imaginal figure until you hear or feel a response. Begin writing at once and write for the other voice. When you are finished with that voice, pause and then respond to it with your own voice. Repeat as often as necessary until the question is answered or your time is finished.

Obstacles

It takes time and practice to hear and feel the voice of an inner figure. Learning this skill takes you to the next level of imaginal work, but it can be frustrating at first. It is important to be patient while learning this skill. Impatience is your worst enemy for it leads to discouragement. In doing this practice, if you feel stuck, go back to the first two exercises and use their methods to stimulate the dialogue and then attempt to hear the voice of the inner figure directly once more.

Conclusion

Continue to work on this practice until you are satisfied that your question was answered and that you made contact with the imaginal figure you chose at the beginning.

_____

CHAPTER 7

Practice 4:
Meeting the Ally

In this practice, you will make use of the method developed in the last practice to meet the ally. For the purpose of this practice I am assuming you have never worked with an ally before. If you have an ally already and know its image and name, you may pick a different intent for this practice. The goal of this practice is to learn something about the ally so if you already know its name and image, ask it to tell you something about itself you do not know. Make learning more about your ally your intent.

In the last practice, you worked with an imaginal figure by dialoguing with it about a specific question. Now you will set up a dialogue with an ally in much the same way, only with a different intent. Your intent is to meet the ally and learn both its form and name. You will try to learn the name of your specific ally and the form in which it will work with you.

By now it is clear that there are many imaginal figures and not all are allies. In order to begin forming a relationship with the ally, it is necessary to know its form. While it is possible to imagine the form of the ally yourself, it is better to let the ally choose its own form. The form in which the ally chooses to appear is significant and meaningful.

The Sufi notion of the "Names" of God can help you appreciate the importance of the image in which the ally discloses itself to you. According to the great Sufi mystic Ibn Arabi, God has many Names, all of which reveal something of Its nature and attributes. The Names are not existent in themselves, but exist only by virtue of being in relationship to all the other Names. All the Names together form an organic whole, which is God. Everything in the cosmos relates back to these Names. The Names, like the imaginal realm, stand between the human being and the reality of the divinity. When we relate to a Name, therefore, we relate to the divinity through the Name.

The ally is a Name, and in fact is a Name capable of including within itself all of the other Names of God. In other words, the ally is in the middle position between its partner and the world of pure divinity, and the ally expresses all the different aspects and attributes of the divinity by the form it manifests as well as by the attributes it displays. The ally can appear in any form and display any attribute because it is capable of being all the Names. Yet we can only experience it as one Name at first and so the form in which it first manifests indicates much about the Name it originally displays. Each person will have a different experience of the ally, for the relationship is unique and because the ally will reveal a different Name to each individual. As the ally work continues, the ally displays many different Names and attributes while usually maintaining the original form in which it appeared. Learning the form in which the ally wishes to appear is important in learning the attributes of your own ally as well as the Name it wishes to reveal to you.

Originally the ally appears in a form that will appeal to its partner or will teach an important lesson. While the ally can change forms at any time, it usually does not do so often. If we recall that the ally acts as a mirror, reflecting back qualities that belong to both the ally and the partner, the form the ally assumes becomes even more significant. If the ally appears as a lion, it is because there is something about this form that is true of not only the ally but its partner as well. It is therefore no accident that the ally appears as a lion and not as a snake. Knowing the right form for the ally opens the possibilities of deeper relationship, of gaining information about the nature of the ally, and learning about your own nature at the same time. It is very important to allow the ally to assume any form it chooses.

The most popular forms for the ally include a big, wild cat, a snake, a dragon, and a horse. Only very rarely does it appear as a humanoid figure, and equally rarely it will appear as an insect. Usually the ally takes on a form that pleases its partner, but sometimes it appears in one that repels him. This makes for a difficult beginning to the ally work but often points out something the partner previously rejected from his or her personality. For example, in one case it appeared as a spider because its partner thought she understood the nature of the ally without having any experiences of it, and the ally wished to appear as an alien with whom the partner had difficulty relating. As they worked, though, and the partner learned how alien the ally could be, she also discovered her own alien nature and came to enjoy it very much. She studied the symbolism of the spider and dialogued with her ally about each of its characteristics until she came to love the spider form. It is hardly ever a good idea to reject the form in which the ally appears, for that is often the ego manipulating your perception, as well as a desire to control the experience, which is counterproductive.

For this practice, therefore, you allow the ally to assume it own form and to reveal its name. You begin the practice by having as your intent meeting your ally and learning its form and name, and you set the stage by asking the ally to come. Your focus consists of expectant waiting with your attention on your thoughts and feelings. Without exercising any control, you simply wait for an image or word to appear. In this practice, you use the technique learned in the previous practice and allow the ally to enter your thoughts when it chooses. Only when you "feel" the form of the ally or find yourself thinking about a specific animal do you write this down. Having felt a specific form, you place your attention on it and imagine being that form as much as possible. You then ask the ally for its name.

By asking the ally for its name, you enter the next phase of the relationship. In the imaginal realm, a name is not a mere appellation but displays the important characteristics of the one who bears that name. In a way, the name of the ally gives you an imaginal definition of the ally, though it may take time to learn the details of this definition. Very often the ally gives itself a name that is not a normal name and may sound incomprehensible and strange. This experience reminds me of the tradition in magic and sorcery in which seemingly meaningless, nonsense names are used for spirits and aspects of the divine. The very strangeness of the name implies that the being so named is different from a human being and that we have no idea of its real nature. This is true for the ally as well, and the strangeness of its name is a reminder of the mystery of its being. This acts as a caution not to imagine that we know the ally if we call it god, angel, or spirit, for that is to define one unknown by another. We can only know the ally by experiencing it and, even then, must accept the ally simultaneously as friend and mystery.

At other times, however, the ally uses ordinary names, such as Peter, Samuel, and David. Even in such cases, the names have meanings which, sooner or later, the ally reveals. Once you have the name, you can use it in several different ways. You can say it repeatedly as in a mantra, knowing the name and the ally are the same. Repeating the name of the ally serves to direct your attention, and consequently energy, to the ally. In future practices, when you wish to focus on the ally, you use either the form or the name to direct your attention.

PRACTICE 4 REVIEW

Find a time and place to do the practice. Make sure you will not be disturbed and, if possible, turn off your phone. It is a good idea to do all of your practices in the same room, and, if possible, at the same time of day. Using the same space and time helps create a ritual for your practice and makes it easier to focus. For the same reason, use the same notebook or journal you wrote in for Practice 1. Having a nice journal with a good feel to it is important. As you now begin work with the ally it might be a good idea to dedicate this journal to that purpose. Choose a question you would like answered and write this down at the top of your page. In this case, it will be a question concerning your ally so your focus will be on the ally.

Intent and Goal

The first intent is to learn the form in which your ally will appear. With this intent, the focus is expectantly waiting while observing your thoughts for a message from the ally. Once you know the form, shift your intent to learning the name of the ally. Focus on the ally's form as you learn its name.

Activity

Write down the intent and center. Wait until you feel or see a form and then ask the ally if that is its form. When you know its form, ask the ally to reveal its name. If you learn this and there is time remaining, begin a dialogue with the ally in order to get to know it better.

Obstacles

It is not always easy to learn the name and form of the ally. Be patient and allow the information to come to you without pushing. The critic may attack the name or the form given to you by the ally, and you may feel foolish about them. As always, ignore the voice of the critic as much as possible. You may have expectations about what the ally should look like. It is important to surrender such expectations and accept any form the ally presents. If it is in any way shocking or disturbing to you, ask the ally why it chose such a form, but do not reject it.

Outcome

Were you successful in contacting your ally? Did you learn its form? What about its name? When you can answer yes to all three questions, move on to the next practice. If you have not yet learned either the form or the name, continue this practice until you do.

CHAPTER 8

Practice 5: Partnership and the Felt Sense

This practice is designed to help you develop a sense of partnership with the ally. At the same time, you shall focus on the felt sense with the aim of developing it. In fact, the felt sense is the most important skill you can develop. Success in its development, in turn, depends on the degree to which you are able to take the ally into your mind. Lending the mind in this way stimulates the felt sense, with the result that, the more you perceive the ally within your mind the more profound the felt sense becomes.

The concept of the felt sense has a long history and has been called many things. In the *Corpus Hermeticum*, a body of work from A.D. 200 attributed to Hermes Trismigestus, we discover that the felt sense was called "Mind." In one of the dialogues of the *Corpus*, the author presents a discussion with what I take to be his ally in which the ally explains about Mind. The ally, called Poimander, first tells Hermes that he can teach him anything he wishes to learn:

> Saying this, he changed his appearance, and in an
> instance everything was immediately opened to me.
> I saw an endless vision in which everything became
> light-clear and joyful—and in seeing the vision I came
> to love.[21]

Poimander symbolizes both the ally and the felt sense
personified. Hermes experiences Poimander as mind, an
accomplishment not explained in the text, but one we can
understand as lending his mind to Poimander. Immediately
the felt sense increased and Hermes began to have visions.
The promise of the ally in this text is that if we lend
our mind to it, the mind expands and perceives reality in
a new and marvelous fashion. It seems that the ally has
the power to perceive and so, when Poimander wishes
Hermes to experience deeper reality, he instructs him
to take him into the mind. When you take the ally into
your mind, or in my conception, lend your mind to the
ally, you deepen your union with it and you discover that
you perceive through the eyes of the ally. You experience
reality in a new way and your felt sense develops more
quickly. By uniting your mind with the ally, you take
on the ability of the ally to perceive reality directly, and
this opens the whole imaginal world to your perceptual
center. Not only do you begin to experience new types
of events, but the depth and quality of your experience
improves. As your felt sense develops, you perceive more
of the ally's reality. As you perceive more, the ally enters
your mind more, and the whole process of development
continues.

It is therefore as if the ally were the perceptual ability you are seeking, so that levels of union correspond with levels of the felt sense. There is nothing more powerful in the development of the felt sense than deepening the relationship with the ally. Since you can consciously work on developing this relationship by asking the ally to help you *feel* more during an imaginal experience, you can focus on developing your felt sense as an exercise. In fact, this is the intent of this practice.

You are entering in to a relationship and partnership with a spiritual being who loves you and wishes you to develop. It will help you grow because it wants and needs you to develop so you can perceive it more clearly. In addition, it wants your consciousness to expand so it can more freely enter your mind. Do not hesitate, therefore, to ask the ally to help you grow and develop your felt sense, for the ally desires this as much as you do. It may not always give you the experience you seek, but it will always take part in your growth. In my workshops, almost everyone who asked was helped by the ally and experienced imaginal reality more deeply simply by asking the ally for help. Asking for a specific experience and reaching it builds trust in the ally and provides a sense that you really are partners.

For this practice, your intent is to experience the Light just as Poimander did. There are several reasons for choosing this experience. The underlying purpose of this practice is to develop the felt sense and to experience partnership with the ally. Light is one of the most interesting symbols in the literature of mysticism and spirituality. We may experience light in many different ways and with many levels of depth. In the East, light is knowledge as well as enlightenment. In the Kabbalah, light streams from the highest levels of the divinity into the universe and our world, and reception of the light connects us with divine consciousness and revelation. In Taoism, light is an energy that we can focus and concentrate in our body. These are but a few of the many meanings of light to be found all over the world. It should be apparent, however, that many of these meanings point to light as an experience. For example, experiencing the light may mean experiencing divine wisdom or the presence of the spirit, the influx of divine energy, or even enlightenment itself. To ask for the experience of light is to invite many possible experiences.

The intent is the experience of light, which may, of course, come in many forms. After first relaxing for a few minutes, invite the ally to come. When you feel its presence, ask it if it will give you an experience of light. Focus on the ally as you imagine it entering your mind and keep your attention on it until you begin to experience the light. Shift your focus to the light and allow the experience to unfold. Your intent is not only to experience the light, but to feel it as deeply as you are able. If, after a few moments, you do not experience the light, check once more with the ally. If it still says it will bring you such an experience, wait patiently. If, for any reason, it refuses, ask it what experience it would like to bring and allow that experience to come. If you do experience the light, keep your focus on it as long as you can.

The point of this practice is not only to gain a felt experience of light, but to explore the nature of the partnership with the ally. You are trying to create an experience with the help of the ally as an expression of your relationship and, even if you do not experience the light, you will gain an awareness of what working with the ally is like. Once you are familiar with this relationship, you will gain confidence in the ability of the two of you to accomplish any goal agreed upon. You cannot impose your will on the ally, but once you are in agreement on a specific goal, you work together to achieve it. More significant than any goal you might achieve is the deepening sense of what union with the ally is like.

Practice 5 Review

Find a time and place to do the practice. Make sure you will not be disturbed and, if possible, turn off your phone. Go to the room in which you practice. Write on the top of your journal page your intention, which is to experience light. Allow the ally to provide any experience of the light it might choose, but stay focused on an experience of light.

Intent and Focus

Your intent is to experience the light in whatever way the ally decides. Focus first on the ally as it enters your awareness, and then on the light. Feel the light as deeply as possible.

Activity

After centering for a few minutes, imagine the name and form of your ally. Imagine it entering your mind. When you feel it enter your mind, ask it if it will give you an experience of the light. Do not try to imagine what this experience might be like, but allow the ally to create any experience it likes. The goal of the practice is to allow the ally to create an experience for you and thus show you what the possibilities of your relationship are. Simply ask the ally to create the experience for you and wait with your focus on the ally. As you begin to experience the light, relax and let the experience unfold, while feeling it as much as possible.

Obstacles

There are two major obstacles in this practice. The first is impatience. Since the goal is to allow the ally to create the experience without any interference, you need to simply wait for the experience. It may take several attempts and you may find yourself becoming impatient or wanting to interfere in the process. Remain as patient as possible and keep trying until you have the experience, or the ally asks you to change your focus.

The second obstacle is mistrust. The point of the practice is to surrender control to your ally, and this may cause fear and anxiety. You may doubt the wisdom of surrendering control to the ally or doubt that the ally is capable of creating the desired experience. In the face of these doubts, stay focussed and patiently await the experience the ally will create.

Conclusion

There are two goals in this practice. The first is to share your mind with the ally and so increase your felt sense. The second is to create an experience of working with the ally. Both goals, when reached, strengthen the relationship with the ally. Allowing the ally greater access to your mind increases the sense of union between you and deepens your felt sense. Achieving a goal together builds trust and a sense of partnership.

Did you experience the light? If so, do you think you felt this experience more than others previously? If you can answer yes to both questions, move on to practice six. If you cannot say yes to both, repeat the exercise until you succeed. Be patient and objective about how the practice went, because this practice leads to progress in ally work and is worth whatever effort it requires. Even if you have succeeded in this practice, you might try it once more with a different goal. Experiment with this practice until you feel deeper trust in the ally and a sense that your partnership is developing.

CHAPTER 9

Practice 6:
Living with the Ally

This practice differs from the previous in that you need not find a secluded spot in which to perform it. In fact, the goal is to experience the ally in the midst of ordinary life.

Every spiritual tradition has a practice for developing union with the inner reality while living in ordinary reality. Buddhists speak of mindfulness, Christian mystics of practicing the presence of God, and Kabbalists of *devekut*. In ally work, this is of special importance. Union with the ally requires that we find a way to be in touch with it at all times, and not simply when we are in meditation. To grow and develop in a robust manner, union must leave the inner rooms and come into life. Developing an awareness that connects you to the ally while you are engaged in daily life is not easy, but the benefits are great and many.

The goal of ally work is to create a shared mind—being aware of the ally's presence in your mind at all times. The usual way that this is expressed is through dialogue and it may be laid down as a general rule of ally work that dialogue is proof that you are in union with the ally. It will therefore be your goal in this practice to engage in dialogue with the ally while being involved in normal life. You should expect to practice for months, if not years, before acquiring the skill necessary to accomplish this goal. I have known many good students of ally work who never accomplished this ability. Others have noted the problem involved in cultivating an on-going awareness of self or other. Many years ago, I attended a lecture by the renowned writer Alan Watts. There were several hundred people in attendance. The talk was interesting but what I remember most was a challenge Watts gave us as we prepared to take a ten minute break. He asked us to remain aware of our centers throughout the ten minute break. As we returned from the break he asked how many people had remained aware of themselves for the whole ten minutes. Only one person raised his hand, to which Watts responded: "You must either be a saint or a liar." I have since learned how right he was. To be aware of yourself or of your ally for ten minutes without a stop is a major achievement.

There is a wonderful Hindu story that illustrates this fact. There was a great sage who had spent many years in disciplines and exercises. Through his efforts, he merited a great boon and the god Vishnu came to him and asked him what great gift he desired. The sage replied that he wished to learn the secret of illusion; of why, in other words, people forget themselves in the flow of life. Vishnu was not happy about this choice and warned the sage that he should choose another request, but the sage insisted. Vishnu finally assented, but told the sage he wished to take a walk with him before starting his explanation. The two walked together out into the country. After a while, Vishnu told the sage that he was thirsty and requested him to go to a well in a nearby village to get him a glass of water. Off the sage went and as he was standing by the well, a beautiful young maiden came up to fill her bucket with the water. The two began to talk and before long they were very taken with each other. The sage walked off with her to her home and in a few months the two were married. They lived happily for many years, raised a family and prospered. Many years later, the sage took a walk and as he approached the spot where he and Vishnu had stood, he saw Vishnu still standing there. Vishnu simply said, "Where is my water?"

The point of the story is not that the sage was wrong in marrying, but that he totally forgets Vishnu. So powerful is the attraction of ordinary life that we forget the inner life completely. For this reason, many spiritual individuals in ages past withdrew from the world in order to be alone and avoid distraction. All too often they discovered, however, that distractions followed them into isolation. Even if such withdrawal worked—which is unlikely—such a choice does not meet the needs of the psyche today, for it requires wholeness and the ability to live both a spiritual and a secular life. One should not be sacrificed for the other. To unite these two worlds, however, requires finding a way to be in relationship with the spiritual while in the day-to-day. To express this solution, the story might have ended with the sage, remembering Vishnu, walking back to him and saying: "Look, I have met this wonderful girl and fallen in love. Come live with us in the village for a while." Bringing Vishnu into the village would unite the worlds and end a perceived split between the spiritual and the worldly.

As I mentioned, dialoguing means being in union, so, if you can learn to dialogue with the ally at any time, you can be in union at any time. Checking in with the ally and having short conversations with it serves to center you all through the day, even when you have not had the opportunity for quiet time. It strengthens the bonds that connect you to the ally and pulls the daily and imaginal worlds together. All in all, continuous dialogue is an important tool in forging union with the ally.

There are *four hints* that I can offer for developing the ability to remain in contact with the ally during ordinary life. *The more time you spend dialoguing with the ally, the easier it becomes to contact the ally at will.* The practices in this book, with daily application, teach you how to shift your focus from ordinary time to the ally. As this skill grows, you can use it at times other than meditation. The key is the ability to shift focus, so the more you practice this shift, the better.

The second hint is to *watch for gaps in the flow of your day.* Usually, one event follows another in rapid succession during the course of the day, but there are always "pauses" in the flow, when events slow down for a time. You might, for example, find yourself alone in your car, or walking to a meeting, resting on a plane, or taking a short coffee break. People who smoke know that often they smoke in order to find just such a break in the flow of their day, but you can find these without smoking. Whenever the empty place in your day appears, seize it and do a short dialogue. Say hello to the ally and ask it how it is or if it has anything to say to you. You can do this in just a few moments. If you have a little more time, close your eyes and imagine that the ally is present with you and place your focus on it. Even if you have trouble feeling the presence of the ally or hearing any response, keep trying. Part of the benefit is learning to shift your focus in a brief time, and you can practice this even if you don't get a response.

The third hint concerns the fact that this *practice is related to mindfulness in general*. If you lose contact with yourself, you cannot retain it with the ally. As Alan Watts knew, mindfulness is hard to develop. One practice is to simply remember to remember. Whenever you think of it, take a moment to remember who you are, where you are and what you are doing. Then go back to your daily activities. This is very simple and you can practice it hundreds of times during the day, but trying it will soon convince you how hard it is to do. Practice as often as you remember to, and when possible, go from this simple remembrance to contacting the ally.

The fourth hint is to *practice remembering yourself or the ally at night as well as during the day*. Try to make contact before going to sleep. At the same time, ask the ally to come into your dreams, and make an effort to dialogue with it if it does. Every time you wake up, remind yourself of yourself and of the ally. Every hint and every practice has to do with shifting focus and paying attention to your center and to the ally. All four could be reduced to one simple statement: Shift your focus to the ally whenever you can.

The obstacles are many, but all ultimately derive from the same cause—the compelling attraction of everyday events. It is too easy to identify with them so completely that we forget the ally. There is nothing wrong with daily activities, unless they consume your awareness and you have no time for spiritual nourishment. In order to get around this obstacle, some people turn away from ordinary life as completely as possible in order to focus on the ally. Although this seems laudable, it creates such an imbalance in a person's life that developing his or her focus becomes all but impossible. As one Zen teacher put it: "Little enlightenment, go to the mountains; big enlightenment go to the city." In other words, a person with a strong focus can stay connected amid the action and distraction of a big city, while those with a weaker focus must go the mountain to protect their connection with the ally. If we opt for the mountain too quickly, we never develop the required focus at all. In my experience, this is not the only deficit from such a choice. Even when almost entirely alone, people may be possessed by daily life, while those in the midst of it may not be overtaken by it at all. It is not a question of withdrawal or denial, but of building a powerful attention. Though it may be harder to do at first in a normal environment, in the long run your focus will be stronger if you have struggled to develop it.

Have your intent clearly in mind and focus on the ally as often as you remember. Try to connect to the ally throughout the day and when you fail, as you certainly will, lay any judgment aside and simply return your focus to the ally.

Though this practice is not easy, remember that you can ask the ally for help. You can make the intent of your day to remember the ally and ask it to contribute to the effort in whatever way it can. Just as in the last practice when you worked with your ally in partnership to experience the light, here you can work together to develop skill at shifting focus. You can shift some of your burden onto your ally, who will be glad to help.

With this practice, you will reach a whole new level of commitment to the ally. The work involved in trying to focus on the ally during the day and night cannot be overestimated. Such work requires a great deal of dedication. Moreover, success requires a transformation in your attention, during which the attention becomes much stronger. The effort and the transformation are so profound that the depth of relationship to the ally becomes apparent. At this point, some people become nervous and wonder if they really want to make such a great commitment. Whether you succeed or not in developing a focus capable of uniting you with the ally all the time, you must ask yourself if you are ready to make the commitment to the ally work that this practice demands.

Practice 6 Review

Preparation for this practice is different from that of the others. Since the goal of the practice is to experience the ally in the daily world, you will not go to your favorite spot. However, you might want to choose a specific time to practice. For example, if you are on an airplane, bus, train, or *riding* in a car (not *driving*, however!) you might take 30 minutes to practice focusing on the ally. Or, if you know you have an extra 10 minutes after lunch, you might try then. For this practice you need not have a specific duration in mind either, since you will try to focus on the ally whenever you can. The best preparation, however, is to remind yourself as often as you can to focus, and hold your focus for as long as you can.

For awareness in your sleep, ask the ally every night before going to sleep for it to appear in your dreams. Write down whatever you remember of this appearance in the morning. Gradually stay aware of the ally when it appears and ignore the rest of the dream.

Intent and Focus

Your intent is to develop the capacity to connect to your ally anywhere and anytime. Ultimately, the goal is to be in relationship with the ally all through the day and night. Specifically, your intent is to shift your attention to the ally during the course of the day and at night. Place your focus on the ally as often as possible.

Activity

Unlike the other practices, you can engage in this one whenever and wherever you wish. Whatever you are doing, and wherever you are, think of the ally or say its name as if it were a mantra. If you have a few moments, close your eyes and call to the ally. Wait quietly, keeping your focus on the ally. Remain focused as long as you can and return to your daily activities. In much the same way, before going to sleep, focus on the ally and ask it to come into your dream. If you have enough awareness in your dream, focus your attention on the ally.

Developing awareness while asleep is as difficult as developing it during daily activities. Being aware in your dream is known as "lucid dreaming," but I do not mean by this term what is often meant. Frequently there is associated with the notion of lucid dreaming the idea of controlling your dream, but that is not the goal of this practice. You do not want to control your dream, but only to be aware as it occurs. Moreover, in this practice, no matter what is happening in your dream, you want to reach out for the ally and turn your attention to it. For many years I had the experience of seeing my ally appear in the middle of a dream that had nothing to do with it. This became almost comical, as if the ally appeared as a character in a play, but in the wrong play. I realized, however, that it wanted my attention, so gradually I practiced remaining aware of what it was doing. In time I felt union with it in my sleep and in dreams of all kinds. This certainly does not happen every night, but when it does it is a beautiful experience.

As in my case, it is easiest in sleep if the ally appears first. To develop the skill of being aware of your ally while dreaming, ask the ally to appear in your dream. Ask it every night before going to sleep, and when it does, try to remember its appearance in the morning. Next, when it appears, try to remain aware of it no matter what else is happening in the dream. Together you and the ally can develop a sense of union that will permeate and, in time, transform your experience of dreaming.

During those periods when you have more time to yourself, practice shifting your awareness between the ally and some other activity, such as reading. Read for a short time and shift your focus to the ally. Pay attention to the ally for a while and then return to your reading.

Ask your ally to partner with you in developing your focus. Work together as a team to develop this skill.

Obstacles

The major obstacle during the day is the compelling fascination of daily events. Without practice, your attention is usually so firmly placed on the world around you that you do not remember the ally. Work slowly and patiently to develop the ability to shift your awareness at will.

The obstacles to connecting with the ally during sleep are all too apparent. Sleep is a deep state of unconsciousness in which awareness is dimmed greatly. Be patient and approach this effort in a playful way. Ask the ally to come into your dreams and try to become aware when dreaming. Lucid dreaming can be great fun, but requires great effort.

Conclusion

Ask yourself if you remembered the ally during the course of the day. When you are able to answer in the affirmative, move on to the next practice. However, this practice is one that you never really outgrow. Return to it as often as you can for its power in creating the union with the ally is great.

Shifting your attention to the ally throughout the day requires on your part a great commitment to create union. You simply can neither succeed at this practice without such commitment, nor can you move on the intermediate practices. Ask yourself, therefore, if you really are willing to commit to the ally in such a manner. Are you sure you want to make this relationship part of you everyday life? Only when you feel such a commitment are you ready to move to the next level of practices.

PART III

Second Coniunctio

CHAPTER 10

Intermediate Practices

Having committed yourself to deepening your relationship with the ally, you are now in a position to move to the next level of ally work. It is the goal of this intermediate stage to develop such a strong connection to the ally that you are aware of its presence most of the time. The previous practice was designed to help you work on this directly, but all the following practices also have as an underlying goal building this kind of relationship. One of the ways of arriving at this goal is to develop your felt perception of the ally. This requires that you not only feel the ally often but that the quality of your feeling transforms as well.

In the Introduction, I pointed out that the depth of feeling corresponds with the "reality" of the experience. By working to increase your felt sense of the ally, you are moving closer to the imaginal level of experience and thereby making the experience more real. There are no limits to the ways and the depths in which you can experience the ally. It always remains a mystery. I have lived and worked with my ally all of my adult life, but it never fails to surprise me with a new feeling experience, or a new insight into its nature. Often when I least expect it, the ally reveals an aspect of itself I never knew. One of the greatest joys I have had in ally work is discovering new properties and aspects of the ally's nature. Since the goal of ally work is relating to and becoming conscious of the ally, the ability to experience new facets of it is essential.

Equally important is the continual development of your capacity to feel. I keep returning to the topic of the felt sense because it carries overwhelming significance in ally work. The more feeling in the experience, the more real it is and the more real the experience, the more transformative impact it has. All progress in ally work depends on developing the felt sense. As the felt sense deepens, you discover different features of the ally that allow you to relate more intimately. Just as in any long-term relationship in which you continually learn more about your partner, you learn more about the ally's nature and consciousness as the relationship develops.

The ally has its own personality and, while it is by no means a human one, it requires development and manifestation. I have spoken of the ally becoming more real, but it also displays different properties. The development of the ally's total personality depends on the ability to perceive it. The great Iranian teachers of the imaginal way realized this and taught a great deal on this subject. For example, according to Henry Corbin,[22] there is a Sufi theory that the subtle body consists of various centers, each of which is an organ of perception. As the perceptual skill of the individual develops, the perceptual centers open, strengthening the subtle body, which offers the individual the promise of a new body after death. Interestingly, however, as the perceptual centers open, the individual gains different perceptions of their angel, or ally, for the angel grows as well. It is as if the very act of perception creates the conditions in which the individual and the ally grow.

This theory has immense importance for ally work. What I term the felt sense corresponds to the perceptual ability represented by the centers in the Sufi concept. As the felt sense develops, three things occur. You have an experience in which you see a new dimension of the ally. As a result of this experience, you transform and develop a new aspect of consciousness and personality. At the same time, the ally grows and gains the ability to manifest new parts of its nature. As both partners grow, they discover that the relationship between them has also developed. The act of perceiving, when it has the felt sense connected with it, is the means by which you and the ally transform, as does the relationship between you.

One of the ways you can experience the development of the relationship to the ally and feel it more profoundly and intimately is through the sharing of your minds. I have spoken of the need to learn how to share your mind with the ally so that it can communicate with you. As ally work deepens, however, the ally begins to share *its* mind with you. The ally's mind is much different than that of a human being, and there is much about it that will remain forever incomprehensible. Nevertheless, when the ally begins to share its mind, you experience visions and thoughts that alter totally your way of seeing reality. It is as if you are looking at the world through the eye of the ally and thought the thoughts of the ally as if they were your own.

To comprehend the mind of the ally is difficult if not impossible, but to comprehend the idea that the ally shares its mind with its human partner is also difficult. I will offer one example to convey the flavor of what I mean. I was once holding a cat that was dying in my lap. I loved the cat very much and was greatly saddened by its dying. As I sat mourning with it, the ally appeared in my mind. "Why are you sad?" the ally asked. "May cat is dying," I told the ally. "Why are you sad?" repeated the ally. "Of course I'm sad because death is a terrible thing to suffer," I replied, becoming angry. "Look at death!" the ally exclaimed, laughing. It was then as if I were suddenly in my ally's mind, watching my cat die, with my ally's eyes, and understanding. I watched as the energy body that was the cat left its body and shifted dimensions (the words do not convey the vision, but I have no better ones). It was a body of light, but I felt it as the exact same essence as my cat. It was not a universal energy but one specific and particular to my cat and I knew it was the essential nature of the cat. I also knew that nothing was ever lost to death and that all beings, great and small, have a unique essence to them that lives forever. As my vision shifted back to normal and I entered my own mind again, the ally repeated to me: "Why are you sad?"

Needless to say, I grew a lot from this experience and still think about it often. By one gesture, sharing its understanding of death with me, the ally opened up a new way of understanding death and the uniqueness of all life. I learned more in those few moments than I would normally learn in a year. As your relationship to the ally deepens, therefore, the possibility of sharing minds with it is one of the most exciting experiences you can have.

CHAPTER 11

Practice 7:
Feeling the Ally

As with all of the most important processes related to ally work, you can ask the ally to help you develop your felt sense. That is what you shall do in this practice. You will ask the ally to help you feel it in a way that you have never done before. Your intent will be to feel the ally in a new way and, at the same time, with more feeling than you have experienced before. With this double intent, your focus is on the ally.

Once you begin the meditation, ask the ally to create a felt experience of something new relating to the ally itself. Focus your attention on the ally and wait. A good way to focus your attention and help create the experience is through dialogue. Talk to the ally about the experience and ask it to describe what it hopes to show you. Keep discussing the experience until it begins. You can then either focus on the experience itself or continue to dialogue with the ally about what is unfolding. In all future practices, when I recommend focussing on the ally, the best way to do so is through dialogue. It is not necessary to know ahead of time what experience the ally plans to create, for the intent is simply to have any new experience it wishes.

You should anticipate the normal resistances. In addition, when feelings increase, fear often occurs. This is natural, for you are moving closer to the psychoid and giving up more control. As much as you think you are ready for such experiences in theory, having them is quite another matter. If you told me you never felt fear in ally work, I would worry. Fear arises when you face something unknown and uncontrollable; if you never feel fear, you aren't reaching the depths of the practice. The question is not *if* you will experience fear but how you will deal with it *when* you do.

If you feel a great deal of fear, stop the practice and center for a short time. When you are ready to begin again, ask your ally about your fear. Most often it is a normal reaction, but occasionally it may indicate that some problem exists. It is a good idea to check with the ally before proceeding in case it is necessary to stop the work for some reason. If for any reason the ally indicates you should not continue, then stop the practice. The next time you approach the ally, ask it to explain what happened and do whatever work is required to deal with it. If, however, it tells you things are fine, then continue to center until you feel ready to try the experience once more.

Do not be surprised by fear, but do not be defeated by it either. Consider it carefully and, when necessary, deal with it, but then return to the work.

PRACTICE 7 REVIEW

Prepare for this practice in the usual way. Find the time and space to practice as you have done previously, but make doubly sure you will not be disturbed as you will be exploring new feelings and experiences that you will not want interrupted. Try to make yourself as relaxed as possible so you do not give in to any fear that might arise and be ready to stop the practice and recenter as often as required.

Intent and Focus

Focus on the ally by engaging in dialogue with it, and have as your intent a new experience of the ally at a more intense level of feeling than you have had before.

Activity

Begin by centering in your accustomed manner. When you are ready, ask the ally to come and, when you feel it is present, ask it to reveal some previously unknown aspect of itself. At the same time, ask it to help you feel the experience more profoundly than ever before.

Leave the details to the ally and continue to dialogue with the ally until the experience begins. Then you may shift your focus to the unfolding experience or continue to dialogue.

Obstacles

As your feelings deepen, it is normal to feel fear because you are getting close to the deeper imaginal spaces. Do not repress your fear but, having taken note of it, continue with the practice. Stop only if the ally indicates there is some problem or the fear grows too strong to ignore.

Outcome

When you are finished, ask yourself if you had a new experience of the ally. Did you also gain a more intense feeling during the practice? If you can answer "yes" to both questions, move on to practice 8. If you say no to either question repeat this practice. The goal of developing a strong felt sense is so important that it is worthwhile to repeat this practice until you are satisfied with the results. It is also a good idea to repeat this practice from time to time.

CHAPTER 12

Practice 8: Knowing Yourself

St. Teresa of Avila said that one must know oneself in order to know God. There are few more profound and dangerous illusions in life than that of having an erroneous self-image. As an analyst, I can testify to importance of self-image and the difficulty involved in changing it. It is a very rare person who has true knowledge of self undistorted by complexes, ambitions, or fear. While many therapists and teachers warn of the dangers of inflation, or having too exalted a sense of self, it is my experience that most people have the opposite problem: They think very little of themselves. I have heard many people say they are unworthy of a certain experience. Holding a negative self-image greatly jeopardizes ally work, for to grow and extend your consciousness to meet the ally as an equal requires confidence and faith in your abilities. It requires, above all, the ability to imagine yourself as the ally's partner.

In the early hermetic work, the *Corpus Hermeticum*, the teacher Hermes puts this well:

> Thus, unless you make yourself equal to god, you cannot understand god; like is understood by like. Make yourself grow to immeasurable immensity, out-leap all body, outstrip all time, become eternity and you will understand god. Having conceived that nothing is impossible to you, consider yourself immortal and able to understand everything, all art, all learning, the temper of every living thing. Go higher than every height, and lower than every depth. Collect in yourself all the sensations of what has been made, of fire and water, dry and wet; be everything at once, on land, and in the sea, in heaven; be not yet born, be in the womb, be young, old, dead, beyond death. And when you have understood all these at once . . . then you can understand god.[23]

This is a wonderful text that illustrates the necessary changes in self-perception that accompany ally work. You imagine yourself differently than previously, and, as the text clearly illustrates, a failure to perceive of yourself as possessed of imaginal power and freedom blocks the capacity to understand the ally. You must imagine yourself as the twin of the ally in order to know the ally. Lingering self-doubt and self-hatred or any form of negative self-perception make it impossible to partner the ally and, fact, make it impossible to know the ally.

People who have too exalted a sense of self will likewise have to free themselves of illusion. In this case, having attributed to themselves power or exalted status of a materialistic sort, some individuals imagine themselves as great or special in some way, because they often have special talent, or good looks, or attributes that mark them as superior to most other people. Rather than imagining that they possess abilities that allow them to see and relate to the ally, they hold to the idea that they are special, different, and superior to all others. Such people tend to be brittle and terrified of making a mistake and thereby proving that they are in fact not superior. They become guarded, condescending, and usually plagued by inner fears and insecurity. Naturally enough, these attributes make it difficult for them to relate to other people or to the ally. You need to be willing to be yourself, in all your imperfections and strengths.

The importance of having a correct self-image stems from the significance you play in ally work. It is to you that the ally relates and if you have either an overly positive or negative perception of yourself, it can damage this relationship. Without a well-developed sense of self free of prejudices, you will see the ally through a distorted lens, because you see yourself with the same distortions. Naturally no one is completely free of complexes and psychic wounds that cloud one's perceptions, but if you are aware of these you can heal them, especially with the ally's help. One of the ways the ally contributes to this healing is through its mirroring of you.

You and the ally are like twins in that you each mirror the other. I know from my teaching experience that people sometimes have trouble understanding the notion of "twinning" in ally work, but it is an important concept. To say that you and the ally are twins does not imply that you are identical, or that you can absorb or be absorbed by the ally. Rather, it means the relationship between you is based on mutual perception. I have already pointed out the importance of the perceptual quality of the ally relationship. When you see the ally, you are also seeing something of yourself, and when the ally sees you, it is seeing itself as well. According to the Sufis, the eye with which you see God is the eye with which God sees Itself. In a non-rational way, the vision of the ally is also the vision of the self. Clearly, if you see yourself with a negative bias, that same prejudice will color your perception of the ally. To know the ally, you must know yourself.

The ally also helps to mirror you by speaking of what it sees in you, both good and bad. The ally will point out your mistakes, as well as reflecting all that is good about you. I have spoken of the sense of being seen and embraced by the ally which is so strong a feeling in ally work. By opening up to this feeling, and allowing the ally's perceptions to penetrate, you will heal most any wound to your self-perception.

Since the ally mirrors you in these ways, it is possible for you to ask that it act as mirror, and this is the point of Practice 8, which focusses on the mirroring capacity of the ally and uses it to help you gain an image of the true self. This is one of the more difficult of the practices because of the human tendency to resist deeper self-knowledge. Those who think poorly of themselves resist any picture that contradicts this assessment. They deny the truth of what the ally shows them or, if forced to accept it, acknowledge that the ally has shown them as they could be, but certainly they are not that yet and may never be. Every experience becomes one more cause for self-rejection. People with too high an opinion of themselves resist learning that they are not as perfect as they believed. If you can steer between these two extremes, learning the truth of who you are can be both encouraging and comforting. Though the ally may indeed point out some flaws, it does so only to help you confront your weaknesses, never simply to criticize. The ally does not judge; it only requests that you develop into the self that you can be.

There are different ways that you may experience the mirroring of the ally. One is to engage the ally in a dialogue in which it explains how it sees you as well as how it sees itself. You set this dialogue up simply by asking the ally to tell how it sees you. You might also ask it why it came to work with you and why it loves you. Questions like these initiate a conversation about who you are and can elicit important information from the ally. It is the way that I recommend you carry out this practice.

Of course, the ally need not answer in words. It may present you with a clear insight into your nature, or use an image to portray something it sees in you. If what you experience is not clear to you, ask the ally for elaboration. It is important in this practice that you learn something entirely unknown about your Self. Just as in Practice 7 you learned something about the ally you did not know previously, in this practice, your aim is a new realization about your Self. Try to be open to whatever the ally brings you and do not imagine that you already know your Self, for, most likely, you do not.

PRACTICE 8 REVIEW

Having centered, invite your ally to join you. Ask it to show you something about your Self you do not know. Dialogue with the ally and ask it how it perceives you and what it likes about you. Keep talking with it until something strikes you as important. Reflect on the new information you have received and discuss it with the ally. Continue the dialogue until you understand what the ally has shown you and you *feel* its truth.

Intent and Focus

Your intent is to learn something new about your Self from the ally. Focus on the ally through dialogue until it reveals the new perception and maintain your focus until you understand the new information.

Obstacles

The moment you decide to look into a mirror and study your reflection, the resistances arise. You may find yourself afraid of what you will learn or already certain that it will be negative. You may instantly find yourself under attack from critical voices and old feelings of insecurity. In the worst case, you may even confuse the voice of your ally with that of a critic.

It is difficult but essential to know yourself. You must be brave enough to risk learning something you do not like; at the same time, remember that the ally is never harsh or critical. It may be forthright but never hostile, so even if it tells you something difficult, it does so with love and compassion. If you find yourself engaged in a dialogue with a harsh or cutting voice, it is not your ally. If you are unsure if it is the ally who has spoken to you, ask. First request that the ally give you a feeling of its presence and love and then ask for its message. Once you have received it, reflect on it with as much objectivity as you can. Ask yourself if it feels right.

If you find yourself adrift in a sea of negativity, stop the practice. Return to it at a later time when you feel more centered.

Outcome

It is always hard to see oneself clearly. But as a result of this practice, you should feel that you know yourself better than you did before and that you have experienced something that the ally has mirrored about you. You have succeeded in this practice when you have learned something about yourself that you did not know before. Most often, this new knowledge helps you to love yourself and have compassion for all that you have experienced in your life. This is a practice you might repeat from time to time, to continue to heal your wounded self-image and to learn more about who you really are. If you feel you have made progress in learning your true nature, you may go to the next practice. Otherwise, continue this practice until you feel you have made progress.

CHAPTER 13

Practice 9: Love and the Ally

The point of these practices is the creation of a relationship with the ally, but sometimes we forget why we are working so hard to establish this relationship. Periodically we need a reminder of what our motive is. Behind all the work we do and all the frustration we put up with lies love; we relate to the ally because we love it and it loves us. If we ever lose sight of this fundamental fact, we risk losing the meaning of what we are doing. From time to time, then, it is a good idea to focus on the love that creates our bond to the ally.

In this practice, therefore, you ask the ally to help you experience the love that connects you. You ask it to show you how it loves you and at the same time you focus on your love for it. The goal you seek is not simply an awareness of love, the emotion, but a felt sense of all the bonds that hold you in the embrace of the ally.

There are many forms of mysticism and many schools of spiritual practice, but some of the most beautiful forms the mystical imagination takes is that of the divine lover. Sufi poetry is one expression of the deep love felt by both human partner and divine lover. Much of the language and imagery of the Sufi poets apply to the relationship with the ally as well. Rumi wrote:

> Love comes sailing through and I scream.
> Love sits beside me like a private supply of itself.
> Love puts away the instruments
> And takes off the silk robes. Our Nakedness
> Together changes me completely.[24]

Of all the mysteries of ally work, this is the most profound: That we could experience so deep a love with the ally. Yet once experienced, this love is unforgettable and undeniable. There is no way to describe such love, but the purpose of Practice 9 is to help you experience it for yourself. Your intent, therefore, is to experience the love of the ally for you but, at the same time, let all of your love for the ally manifest as well. In a real sense, this is the most important practice you can do and it is a good idea to return to it no matter how far in ally work you go.

PRACTICE 9 REVIEW

Prepare for this practice as usual. Find the time and place to do your writing. Since this practice is about love, you should approach it when you feel open to receiving love and not if you are in a disturbed or angry mood. Center for as long as it takes to relax and feel receptive, and then begin the practice.

Intent and Focus

Your intent is to experience the love of the ally and your focus is on the ally and then on the feeling of love. Speak with the ally about love and, as the feeling manifests, focus on it as completely as possible. At the same time, be open to your own feelings and let your own love manifest. If you do not experience such feelings, remain in dialogue with the ally and ask it why you don't feel its love.

Activity

Having relaxed, ask your ally to talk with you about love and the love that exists between the two of you. After some discussion, ask it to let you feel its love. Keep dialoguing until you feel its love and then focus on that feeling. Open to the feeling as much as possible and remain focused on it for the duration of the exercise.

Obstacles

If you have any issues about trust and relationship, they will arise at this point, if they have not already. Often individuals find it difficult to receive the ally's love or to believe that it is real. Many find it easier to accept criticism than love. At first the love of the ally is so intense as to be painful, and it may be difficult to remain open to it. It is important to stay as open as possible to receiving this love. Imagine it flowing into you and washing away all obstacles and doubt, until the only thing that remains is love itself.

Outcome

Ask yourself if you felt the ally's love and what your reaction to it was. If you experienced it and opened to it, move on to Practice 10. Return to this one as often as possible to be nourished by the love of the ally. If you did not experience the ally's love, repeat this practice. Keep at it until you succeed.

CHAPTER 14

Practice 10:
Caring for the Ally

This is the last intermediate practice. Having made it this far, you have explored relationship with the ally in a variety of ways and gained some essential skills in ally work. In the next section we shall build on these skills as we enter more deeply into felt experience and move closer to the psychoid world. To close this section, however, you shall use a focus that reminds you that being in a partnership with the ally obligates you to care for the ally and abandon the simplistic idea that ally work is for your sake alone. In Practice 9, you experienced the love of the ally as well as your love for the ally. The ally is capable of deep feeling and, perhaps more remarkable, has needs as well. Many people involved in ally work have trouble recognizing that the ally has needs. There is still a tendency to attribute perfection to the ally, for so strong is the belief that God is perfect and complete that it is hard to escape this conviction. Yet, in its own way, the ally indeed has needs. You have already seen that it needs attention in order to grow. The ally can also require certain changes in your life, in attitudes and behaviors, if these block or hinder your relationship with it. It can ask you to initiate something new in both your lives, or give you an intent in your meditation. Whatever the ally needs, however, it is important that you consider these needs and make every attempt to satisfy them. If you take the time to ask the ally what it might need, it reminds you that the relationship is a partnership and its goals are not restricted to what you might want. The goals and needs of the ally must be at least as important as your own.

The greatest error, and one which, unfortunately, is very common, is to imagine that the ally relationship exists solely for your benefit. I hear complaints from students all too frequently that something went wrong with their plans or they became ill or something bad happened. How, they ask, could such things happen if they had an ally? People suppose that having an ally is akin to having a genii in a bottle who will answer their every demand and satisfy their every wish. What a shock it is for these people to learn that the ally might not be interested in creating some sort of paradise for them. Life is about growth and transformation and not about living in ease and comfort. The ally does not seek to take its partner's problems away but to create mutual transformation and growth. Though it is true that the ally, in cooperation with its partner, can create the most extraordinary results in the outer world, this is not its goal. Hard as it is for the human ego to comprehend, the ally does not exist for its manipulation.

It is important to keep in mind the love that exists in the relationship when working with the current practice. If you recall that love is the primary goal and meaning of ally work, it is easier to focus on the needs of your beloved.

The focus of Practice 10, then, is to ask the ally what it wants from you. Your task is to discover what the ally needs and then to focus on obtaining it during the rest of the practice. Whatever the request turns out to be, dialogue with the ally about the task. Ask why it wants this particular thing and how you might go about obtaining or producing it. Consider the request carefully and decide if this is something that feels correct to you. If you have doubts or negative feelings, be honest and share them with your ally. Discuss it all with the ally and then decide what response to make. It is important to be honest. Do not promise what you will not give and do not give what feels wrong. At the same time, do not simply refuse. Be willing to dialogue with the ally until you both reach what feels to be the correct resolution. As soon as you have a sense of what you wish to do, proceed with the intent of giving the ally what it has requested.

PRACTICE 10 REVIEW

Prepare for this practice as usual. Find the time and place to do your writing. Since this practice concerns your ally's wants, put aside your own questions or issues. If you have a burning issue that weighs on you, do not try this practice. Instead, talk to the ally about your issue. You should attempt this practice when you are able to focus on the ally without distractions by your own concerns. When you feel open to the ally's needs, begin the practice.

Intent and Focus

Your first intent is to discover what the ally wishes from you. Having determined that, shift your intent to the goal the ally gave and focus accordingly.

Activity

When you are with your ally, ask it if there is anything it would like to request from you. If there is, discuss it at length until you are clear about what response you wish to make to this request. It may take several sessions to reach this point or you may arrive there quickly. As soon as you know what the ally wants and you are decided to help it gain that result, focus on the response in question. For example, if your ally asks you to help it transform in some way, focus on the ally with the intent to create its transformation. In this fashion, the intent of the practice is whatever the ally wishes and you focus accordingly. Rather than you choosing an intent, therefore, you allow the ally to do so, so long as it feels comfortable and correct. Work together to achieve this intent.

Obstacles

It is easy to fall into the habit of discussing your needs and desires every chance you get and forget the ally's needs. Since the ally work is not just about you but about the relationship between you and the ally it is important to consider the ally's desires as well. When you do finally consider the ally as an equal partner in the relationship, do not be surprised at how many resistances spring into action. You will find yourself resenting the time spent on your ally or having to work for something you might not think important or desirable. Your ego will balk at having to surrender its control and at not being the focus of the ally's attention. No matter how adult we like to think ourselves, the infantile is never far away. Remind yourself of the love between you and the ally and commit yourself to the practice until you have achieved the intent that the ally gave you. Be neither distracted nor deterred by any selfish impulse.

Outcome

The question of outcome is simple: Did you accomplish the goal that the ally gave you or not? If not, keep trying until you do. If you did, move on to Practice 11. It is, however, a good idea to repeat Practice 10 every so often just to remind yourself of the importance of the relationship and the value of considering the ally as an equal partner.

PART IV

Advanced Practices

CHAPTER 15

Empowering the Ally's Voice

As I sit to write this new part on advanced practices I am forced to admit that I do not know what qualifies a person as "advanced" in ally work. The longer I travel this way, the more it stretches out before me. The more accomplished I feel, the more I am presented with difficulties and new challenges to master. I already have in mind the next book, which I should perhaps call *Really Advanced Ally Work*. In all seriousness, there is no end to the ally work you can experience, so if you have made it this far in this book, it is wise not to consider yourself too advanced. On the other hand, if you have travelled this far, then you have accomplished a great deal and should be proud of yourself. In this section I shall challenge you to sharpen your skills even further in order to experience a new level of reality.

In particular, you are going to focus on the voice of the ally in order to empower it in a number of ways. In order to illustrate the value of these practices, I shall use

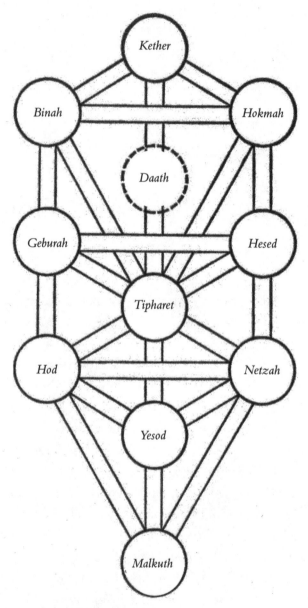

Figure 1. Sefirotic Tree of Life.

Kabbalistic imagery. Kabbalah consists of many different systems, with many of them presenting what might be termed a "mysticism of the word." You can play with letters and words and combine them in certain ways to create both mystical experiences and insight into divine wisdom. Prophecy, which at its highest level consists of letting a spiritual voice speak through you, is considered one of the highest states imaginable. In the Bible, of course, God creates with a spoken word, and so words were considered to hold great power. The tradition of the word and the voice influenced the Kabbalah in many ways and we find in one of its most sacred texts, the Zohar, many uses of the idea of voice. Since you will soon work with the voice of the ally in some special ways, it is interesting to note the way the Kabbalah creates a model for understanding the divine voice.

The central image in the Kabbalah is the divine tree as shown in Figure 1 on page 148. The sefiroth, or columns of the tree, are divine beings with a number of attributes. The Kabbalah gives the sefiroth multiple attributions. For example, Hokmah is both wisdom and mind, and Tiphareth is both king and voice, while the lowest sefiroth, Malkuth, is both kingdom and speech. For our purposes, the interplay between mind, voice, and speech is of great interest.

It must be remembered that the Kabbalah speaks of a God who has broken apart. There are splits within the tree that must be healed to end evil and transmute God into a more perfect state. One of the ways that the split in the tree may be healed is to unite the mind with the voice and the voice with speech. There is much that can be said about this model, but of most interest is the relationship that exists between speech and the divine mind, with voice as the intermediary.

The mind of God is the secret core of the divine, whose depths cannot be fathomed. Few indeed could rise to this level of divinity in order to experience the secrets of the divine mind. But fortunately it is not necessary to ascend all the way to the mind, for the mind is connected to the voice that expresses it. The voice, at the very center of the tree, manifests the mind of God silently as if to keep the secret a little while longer. Voice, however, in its turn, connects to speech, which manifests voice aloud, no longer silently. If this unification occurs, with speech reaching voice and voice touching mind, the whole tree is unified and speech expresses the divine mind. In the Kabbalah, all three—mind, voice, and speech—are parts of the divine totality and the speech that expresses itself aloud is the feminine aspect of God.

Using this model we can say that the ally is in touch with the higher realms of divinity that pass beyond our vision, and that the voice of the ally expresses the divine mind itself. When we speak with the ally, therefore, we are in touch with the mind of God, which expresses itself through the ally's voice. When, therefore, we strengthen the power of the voice, we are uniting God still further and allowing the secrets of the divine mind to pass freely into our world and our soul. Empowering the voice of the ally to the point at which you can hear it easily and in which it spontaneously speaks and communicates itself clearly grants you access to the divine mind and brings its wisdom into your level of reality.

By cultivating the dialogue as you have throughout all the practices in this book, you have empowered the voice of the ally, which is what you shall continue to do. The word spoken to you by the ally in such dialogues carries with it the divine mind. The word is, therefore, a very powerful tool and equally powerful experience. The more power the word contains, the more the divine mind is revealed to us. It is therefore of obvious importance for you to work with the ally in increasing the power of the word.

What is meant by the power of the word? Since the word is the vehicle of the divine manifestation, it is also the vessel into which the divine mind pours itself. If we can increase the holding power of this vessel, it will carry more of the divine into our hearts. It was believed, in the Hermetic tradition, that the devotion and ritual practice of people could impart a divine life to a statue, incarnating the divine being within the statue itself. There is truth in this supposition insofar as it is applied to imaginal reality. The same is true of the word, which your attention and the power of your ally bring to life as the form in which divine energy resides. Moreover, the word is the means by which the divine mind reveals itself to us. You have already seen the importance of the felt sense in deepening your experience of the ally. The same principle applies to the word with which the ally speaks. If you feel the word more intensely, it conveys much more to you—not only in meaning but in impact. You can therefore imagine the word as a vessel capable of holding an infinite amount of the divine Mind as well as having the capacity to communicate this at the level at which you can receive it. If you do not have a felt sense of the word, you only receive a fraction of what you could. The more you develop your felt sense of the word, the more you experience the divine Mind.

The present practice is designed to increase your felt sense of the word spoken by the ally. To achieve this goal, you and your ally need to work together. I have designed several practices useful in this regard. In addition, there are several dimensions of the word which you will develop. The first is clarity. When the ally first speaks with you, it is often hard to hear and feel in your mind, but as its clarity increases, it becomes easier to hear and very hard to deceive yourself about what you heard. The ally speaks without hesitation and long pauses and it becomes easier to understand what the ally means in what it is saying. You hear more easily and you understand with less difficulty.

Words convey not only information, but lead to experiences and states. As the power of the word increases, you feel the experience that the word conveys—the words produce in you that which they convey. If, for example, the ally says be healed, then you are healed. The words carry the experience they express so that hearing the word and having the experience are simultaneous. Moreover, as previously noted, there is a way in which the ally incarnates in its words; it is as if the word contains the energy and essence of the ally so you are able to feel the ally in the words.

Before moving on to the next practice, let us consider an important issue that advanced ally work raises: power. I discussed the question of power briefly in chapter 2 (see page 35) but it is important enough to warrant more discussion. It is wrong to either fear or crave power. Power, like electricity, is a dangerous force that, if used carefully, anyone can use for many good purposes.

The question of power becomes important at this stage of the ally work because words have the power not only to communicate about experience but to create the experience itself. To give another example, at the beginning of ally work, the ally might say to you it wants you to experience love. You might then work on love as your intent. As the felt power of the word increases, however, the ally might say; "Feel my love," with the immediate result that you do in fact experience it. The words spoken create the experience spoken of. Because of the power the ally invests in its words and the development of your felt experience of the words, you gain the ability, in cooperation with the ally, to experience almost any result you choose. Whether you desire it or not, this means you have power. In the ally you have an instrument of great power and the issue of appropriate use of that power takes on great significance.

All traditions, from shamanism to alchemy, grappled with the question of power and have come to their own conclusions. If we examine the view of power in alchemy, we learn that the Philosopher's Stone consisted of the union of love and power. The alchemists were in no doubt about the power of the stone. *The Book of Lambspring* stated that the Philosopher's Stone possessed the power of the whole world[25] and *The Emerald Tablet* went further in stating that the Stone is the cause of all perfection in the world and is perfection itself.[26] It causes transformation and healing and imparts both wisdom and longevity (not to say immortality!). Clearly, to possess the Stone was to possess an instrument of potent transformative power, which could be used to attain wisdom or riches. The alchemists were not always free of the desire to use the Stone for selfish motives, but as a philosophy and spiritual tradition, alchemy insisted that power be united with love.

The union of power with love means that love tames power and insures that it is used for the proper reasons. Practically this means you must always consult the ally before attempting to achieve a particular goal. If the ally demurs, you must be willing to sacrifice this goal. If you are so willing, love holds power in check. However, if you try to achieve the goal despite the ally's caution, power is gaining the upper hand and you should examine how you are dealing with it. On the other hand, you should not dismiss all power. As you have seen, the ally has needs, too, and it might require a great deal of power to satisfy those needs. If you refuse to put in the effort required and desire only to focus on the ally, love might be dominating power. It seems odd to think you might have too much love, but real love requires a willingness to put your energy where it is most needed. At times that might mean focusing and using power to achieve certain goals.

CHAPTER 16

Practice 11: Empowering Dialogue

The power of the word includes clarity, creation of a state or process, and the presence of the ally. The following exercises deal with each of these three aspects as we work on increasing the felt sense of the word. The intent of each of them is the same, but with a different focus. These exercises are only possible at an advanced level because it is important that you already have a relationship with the ally and are able to recognize its voice. The task involved is not to change the voice of the ally but to deepen your experience of it.

Developing the felt sense of the word is important if you are to deepen your ally work. I divide this practice into three exercises but I am presenting them as part of one practice because they are so interwoven and related. It is a good idea to move between them, first practicing one, then another and then the last. Move back and forth until you have achieved mastery of all three. As your skill in one area deepens, it will affect the others as well.

Exercise A:
Developing the Ally's Voice

In preparation for this exercise, go to your accustomed spot, after having freed up enough time to complete it. This exercise may be frustrating as it takes time to hear the ally clearly respond to a direct question. Be as relaxed as you can be and in no rush to complete the exercise.

Intent and Focus

The intent is to engage the ally in a discussion that clearly answers your question. Your focus is on the voice of the ally. You are aiming to experience the clarity of the ally's voice with as little difficulty as possible.

Activity

In this first part of the exercise, you will ask the ally a question that is particularly interesting to you. The goal of this exercise is to receive a clear and authoritative answer from the ally. By the end of the discussion, you should feel satisfied that the question has been answered clearly.

Obstacles

The primary difficulty encountered in this exercise is the difficulty the ally may experience in answering you clearly. The reason you must practice this skill is not only to develop a keener felt sense but to help the ally develop the power of its voice as well. As you begin this part of the ally work you may discover that the ally does not yet have a strong enough voice to do this. If this is the case, be patient and work with the ally in this way until its voice develops. You can tell when this is happening as the experience of the dialogue will change. The ally's voice becomes more fluid and spontaneous, and the words seem to have their own flow. Talk to your ally about the process and about the ways in which you may help it. Recall Practice 10, in which you focused on something the ally needed. This may be the case in the current exercise as well, depending on how developed the ally's voice has become. As you work with the ally on this obstacle, make your intent the strengthening of the ally's voice.

Outcome

If you feel satisfied that the ally answered your question clearly, and that its voice has gotten stronger, move on to Exercise B. Otherwise, keep working with the ally on this question until you feel you have a satisfactory answer before turning to the next exercise.

Exercise B:
Empowering the Word

Having made time and space for this exercise, relax deeply. In this exercise, because you will be experimenting with new experiences and even new states of consciousness, it is important to be comfortable and calm. This is not an exercise to try when agitated or overly concerned with some problem. You must be able to surrender to the experience as completely as possible. It might be a good idea to allow more time for meditating before beginning the exercise, as the deeper into yourself you are able to go, the easier it will be to let the new experience begin.

Intent and Focus

Your intent is to empower the word of the ally and to create a new imaginal experience. Keep your focus on the words of the ally until the experience begins when you shift it to the experience itself.

Activity

In this exercise, you experiment with the power of the word to create experience. It is a simple exercise to describe but a difficult one to achieve. Begin by asking the ally if it is willing to help create an experience with you. It can be one of your own choosing or you can ask the ally to choose, but it should be a new experience. You can ask for an ecstatic experience, a vision, or perhaps an out-of-body journey. Clearly, these are not ordinary states of consciousness and you cannot expect to achieve them in one session. But the intent is to create an unusual perception of reality and to move into imaginal spaces previously unexplored. It is important that you do not work to gain these experiences in any other way than through dialogue with the ally. The real intent is to experience the power of the word to create experience. At some point in the dialogue with the ally, ask it to use the word to create the state in question. Typically, the ally will talk about this state or say something to induce it, but the words spoken by the ally should lead to the experience itself. Pay attention to the words spoken by the ally; they are your focus. Once the ally begins speaking, relax and keep your focus on the words. If an experience begins, change your focus to the experience. Typically with such deep states you will discover yourself moving into a new imaginal space and then, after only a few seconds, lose it and return to normal awareness. Keep trying until you gain the desired result. Be prepared to work on this exercise for weeks or even months if necessary. Keep in mind that, even if you are not having the experience, you are empowering the words of the ally.

Do not give up or ask for a different experience until you feel you have succeeded. You may discover that you have the experience when you least expect it. You might have it in a dream or in the middle of the night or at some unexpected time when you are in a relaxed state. Though the experience may not come in the exercise session it certainly is a result of your work with the ally. Talk about your experience the next time you dialogue with the ally and see what more you can learn. You can at that time move on the next exercise.

If you experience repeated frustration, go back to an earlier exercise and stay there for a while. Return when you feel ready, and try this one again. I do not advise moving on to a new exercise before you succeed in this one.

Obstacles

Fear can be a major obstacle in this exercise. In order to succeed you must let go of control and move into a place that is new and foreign. Much as we may want such a deep experience we also fear the loss of control involved in having it. Success requires a great deal of trust in the ally. Practice relaxing as you find yourself entering imaginal space and be patient as it may take some time to overcome your fear. If you find it too difficult to let go of your control, dialogue with the ally about what you are feeling.

Since we have now entered the deeper aspects of ally work, you may also discover that, as the experience commences, you cannot remain still and find yourself agitated. The body often has a reaction to moving deeper into imaginal space, much like a skittish horse nearing a cliff. Try to relax, but if you cannot, stop the exercise and center. Return to it later. Learning to abandon yourself to an experience you cannot control takes time, and the fear of such abandon forms the principle obstacle to this exercise.

Outcome

When you feel your ally has created an experience through its word you may move on to Exercise C. If you are not sure, or believe it has not, repeat this exercise until you are certain that the experience-through-word has been reached, at which point you can move on to the next exercise. Do not move on until you have attained the goal of this exercise. If you feel stymied and unable to complete it, return to some earlier practices for a time and then try this one once more.

EXERCISE C:
THE ALLY IN THE WORD

This exercise focuses on the ability of the ally to express itself in word. You have just worked with a process through which the word of the ally creates an experience. The words used by the ally also carry a felt sense, just as a visual image does. In this case, the words convey the felt sense of the ally itself: its nature, attributes, personality, and presence. In the act of hearing the word, you feel the ally. Thus, when you are in a dialogue with the ally, you feel its essential self. It does not matter what words the ally uses in this regard, for it is the felt sense contained in the word that matters. As you hear the words, you feel something difficult to define but which is unmistakably ally. You can never mistake who is speaking, for the words bring the presence of the ally before you. It is a very intimate experience that permits you to experience an inner dimension of the ally.

Preparation for this exercise is the same as previous ones. Find the right spot and time and relax deeply. You will be working with the felt sense in this exercise so be ready to shift from thinking to feeling. Quiet your mind as much as possible and open to any felt sense that might appear, no matter how small.

Intent and Focus

Your intent is to feel the ally in the words spoken to you. Focus on the ally and what it is saying, but focus especially on any feelings that you might notice. If a feeling becomes clear, shift your full attention onto the feeling. Sit with your attention on this feeling as long as you can.

Activity

The point of this exercise is to experience the felt quality of words. As the ally speaks, you feel its essence
and its other attributes while listening to its words.
In performing this exercise, therefore, engage in a
dialogue with the ally about anything you like. As you
dialogue, though, pay attention to how the words make
you feel. Try to feel the presence of the ally in them.
See if you are able to discern anything more about
the ally as you dialogue. Let the words flow over you
while you monitor the feelings they create within you.
When you write, note not only the words spoken but
the felt sense you have of the ally.

Obstacles

When you experience new feelings, you may experience fear as I mentioned in the last exercise. Usually
the feeling connected with the word is positive and
powerful, but being unknown may nevertheless trig-
ger fear. As always with fear, work your way through
it while continuing the exercise. If the fear becomes
overwhelming, stop and center; return to the exercise
or wait until your next practice.

More common than fear is impatience. It may take
some time and effort before you notice the power in
the words. Be patient, because the ally must develop
the ability to manifest in the word and the purpose

of this exercise is to give it the opportunity to do so. If you practice for some time and still nothing has changed, you might ask the ally what the reason is. If there is any problem or block it will let you know, but, most often, the ally is still working on developing a new skill.

Outcome

Once you have experienced a special sense or feel of the words spoken by the ally you may move to Practice 12. From this point on, however, when you do a dialogue with the ally, pay close attention not only to the words but the feelings related to them. You can work on developing the power of the word in every practice that you do. The more power the words accumulate, the more powerfully the ally manifests. If you experience difficulty developing this skill, maintain your efforts, but return to earlier practices for a period of time. Do not move on to Practice 12 until you feel satisfied with your efforts with this one.

CHAPTER 17

Practice 12:
The Ally and Friends

The imaginal world is home to entities other than the ally. While the exploration of this realm and the investigation into the relationship between the ally and other entities is relatively new, two facts are apparent. The ally is different from other entities in that it tends to organize the others around itself as center. Much as the Self acts in the psyche to harmonize all the complex and archetypal energies, the ally acts to organize the other imaginal forces. In its interaction with these forces, then, it plays a special role and does not simply act as the others do. In one other way it evidences a difference as well; the ally grows when it interacts with other imaginal forces, as if it were taking the energy from the other into itself. When the ally and imaginal entities relate, the ally grows and regulates the others.

In alchemy there are symbols that correlate with and help elucidate the role of the ally and the reason it grows from contacts with other entities. The Philosopher's Stone grows when it contacts spiritual forces of heaven and earth. The alchemist can actually feed the Stone in a process called *cibatio* and in the *sublimatio* and *multiplicatio* we find other parallels for the ally's conversion of energies.

The Stone, once created, adds to itself the power or "virtue" of all other substances and powers. Through the process of the *multiplicatio,* the power of the Stone will "multiply to infinity in the same way, the first over ten, the second over a hundred, the third over a thousand, the fourth over ten thousand, and as follows you will obtain accordingly to infinity, always following the same way."[27] Georg Stahl assures his readers that the *multiplicatio* not only increases the quantity of the Stone but also increases Its quality.[28] Nicholas Flammel, an early alchemist of the fourteenth century, presented a more complete picture of the *multiplicatio*:

> *Multiply* the budding and increasing natures; for look how often thou shall dissolve and fix, so often will these natures multiply in *quantity, quality,* and *virtue,* according to the multiplication of *ten*: coming from this number to an *hundred,* from an *hundred* to a *thousand,* from a *thousand* to *ten thousand,* from *ten thousand* to an *hundred thousand,* from an *hundred thousand* to a *million,* and from thence by the same operation to *Infinity. . .*[29]

The operation of the *multiplicatio* is the one with which we are concerned during this practice. As the alchemists explain, having obtained an ally and created a relationship

Figure 2. The newly-created Stone ascends to the higher mountain and contemplates the stars. From *The Book of Lambspring.*

with it, you now enter upon the immense task of multiplying the power, nature, and consciousness of the ally. I explained earlier how the ally might grow in power, and the focus of ally work now centers on the transformation and development of the ally almost exclusively. As Flammel said, the process of development may go on to infinity, as the ally never exhausts its potential for growth. Your focus and intent is on this infinite development of the ally's nature.

As you participate in the growth of the ally, you experience a continuous growth process. Even though the goal is not your own growth but of the one that you love, you participate in this development nevertheless.

The emblem in Figure 2 on page 169 depicts the sublimation process in which the newly-created Stone ascends to the highest mountain and contemplates the stars and their powers. But, as the radiating energy pouring from the stars reveals, the Stone does not just contemplate the stars but takes their energy into Itself, transmuting their energies into Its own. The same occurs in ally work in a process I call conversion, in which imaginal energies of all kinds are ingested by the ally and converted into itself, triggering a powerful process of transformation. It is impossible to tell beforehand just what change will occur in the ally, but there is no doubt that some change does indeed occur.

The last practice I shall present is therefore devoted to creating a change within the ally by means of the conversion of imaginal energies. At this stage of ally work, the human partner can do little to create the outcome of a process but hold the intent. The rest is up to the ally. If you have not yet experienced it you will at this point understand what it means to ride the untamed dragon that the ally is, for the journey you embark upon in this practice is totally out of your control. All you do is hold on to the ally and to your focus.

You may break the actual practice into two main parts. First, experiencing another imaginal entity and, second, the conversion of its energies into the ally. In the first part of the practice, you ask the ally to introduce you to an imaginal figure. It may be any figure that you or the ally choose but, as always, it should be one that you find of great interest. You may have dreamed about it or read of it in a book, but in any case you should have a definite figure in mind when you begin. First invite your ally to be present with you. Then invite the other figure to come. Begin to dialogue with it as you would the ally. Learn everything you can about the figure and dialogue with it over the course of several sessions or until you feel you know all you wish to. When you are satisfied that you are finished with dialoguing with the figure, ask the ally if it is ready to try to convert some of the energies of the figure. If it is, you may begin the second part of this practice, which involves conversion. I cannot tell you how this process will proceed for there are many variables influencing outcome and development, and at this stage of the work your ally is uniquely your own. Ask the ally to begin the process of conversion and keep your focus on both the ally and the other figure. Your intent now is to experience the transference of energy from the figure to the ally. Keep focussed on both, but you must now await the ally. Only the ally can engage in this process. At some point, you will feel something happening at the energetic level. You may perceive it as a transformation of energy or the split-second blaze of light. However you perceive it, you should feel that the transfer has occurred. That is the time to close the session. When you do the next one, ask the ally to show you the energy converted and what change it has produced within the ally. Whatever happened, the ally grew from the experience. When you recognize that the ally has changed, and it indicates to you the nature of the change, the practice is over.

The dynamic by which the ally transforms and influences the imaginal world is significant and deserves more study. This practice integrates one of the secrets of alchemy and puts it to use in ally work.

Needless to say, the nature of this practice is more complex than others that preceded it. There are more steps involving different intents and foci than previously. There are more goals to achieve as well. There are three primary goals associated with this practice. The first is to increase your awareness of the universe and the entities and figures that exist within it. Dialoguing with other imaginal figures is a stimulating learning experience and can yield previously undreamed of insights. So powerful are these figures that you must be careful not to lose your position and standpoint by falling under the influence of the figure. No matter how compelling the information received from the figure, check it out with your ally and sit with it at least one session before trying to follow or integrate it.

The other danger is more subtle. These entities are often numinous and elicit strong feelings, so you must be careful they do not overwhelm you. No matter how wise, beautiful, or numinous the figure, resist the urge to worship or surrender to them. The purpose of ally work is to empower the ally, and to do so you must experience other profound figures, but if you give up your autonomy to them, you will no longer be able to do ally work. This may not seem like a real threat, but it is. It is best not to underestimate the power of the imaginal figures. Such subversions can occur and, before giving over to them, remember to ask your ally about what you feel. The best protection from such excessive feelings lies in keeping your boundaries intact and knowing when to stop the practice.

Imaginal beings are energetic, and if you encounter this figure at an objective level you need to protect yourself from the energy. You could become manic, agitated, or generally unwell if you receive too much energy. It is not always possible to control what happens in an experience, but if you have had an energetic experience, rest and monitor your body for a few days. If during the experience you find yourself dizzy or disoriented, stop the practice.

One of the most common experiences people have when contacting figures deep within the imaginal realm has to do with vibrations. When in the presence of an imaginal being, people often speak of feeling vibrations in their body, or seeing them in the air around them. The vibrations can be distressing but are not dangerous and are a good sign that you are having a deep experience. Do not, therefore, be bothered by vibrations unless they prove too overwhelming.

The second goal of the practice is to transform the ally by converting some of the energy of the other entity. This alchemical process occurs whenever the ally engages with another imaginal figure and you need do nothing to make it happen. Your only task is to dialogue with both ally and entity and to perceive the changes as they occur. The ally is capable of infinite growth and each time you dialogue with it, you feed it. Alchemical conversion, however, is a much more dramatic stimulation of the ally's growth. The effects of the process are so intense that you may experience it only rarely. It is as if the ally has to digest what it has gained before it is ready to convert any more. It is therefore advisable not to do this practice too frequently. You may return to it several months after a successful experience.

The third goal is to bring harmony to an otherwise chaotic realm. As the ally converts energy from a psychoidal entity, it also brings it into relationship. The ally, united with its partner, serves as a center around which other imaginal figures may organize. As in alchemy and the Kabbalah, one of the goals of ally work is bringing order to the chaos of the universe.

Practice 12 Review

Intent And Focus

Your first intent is to meet a psychoidal being, to dialogue with it, and to learn what you can. Your second intent is to convert energy belonging to the being into the ally. You need to focus on both the ally and the other entity and keep them both in your field of attention until the exchange of energy occurs.

Activity

Much may be accomplished in this practice, and it is necessarily complex. At the practical level, however, it is not much changed from earlier ones. Relax and contact your ally. Ask it to introduce you to another imaginal figure. Once contact has been made, engage this figure in dialogue. It is important to remain aware of your ally as you dialogue with the other figure. You must, therefore, be aware of two figures at the same time. Dialogue with the figure for several sessions until you have learned some things from it, and then ask your ally if it wishes to try conversion. If it does, then make your intent conversion of energy from the figure to the ally, and focus on both figures. Conversion will not occur unless you experience it. You will know when it has happened, for there is a definite, though hard to describe, sensation associated with it. You may see a flash of light, enter an ecstatic state, or simply have a felt sense that energy has passed into the ally. Frequently, a process of change then occurs for the ally, and you should notice some differences in your ally over the following weeks.

If nothing happens in the session, return to the practice again later. Be patient and remember it is up to the ally to accomplish this intent.

Obstacles

There are several obstacles you might encounter in this practice. The major one is experiencing physical effects from the encounter with the imaginal figure. This might take the form of dizziness, a sense of paralysis, or disturbing vibrations. These are not normally harmful but if they are disturbing it is a good idea to stop the practice.

The other danger is more subtle. These entities are very powerful and numinous and you may find yourself irresistibly drawn to the feeling of numinosity they generate. If you simply surrender to this feeling, you may find yourself under the influence of this entity. Though they usually are wise and helpful, they are not the ally and never act as an ally. They do not devote themselves to an individual but to their own purposes, which may or may not correspond to what is good for you. Moreover, if you lose your sense of autonomy, it will very difficult to integrate what you learn from the entity. It is best, therefore, to let your ally run interference for you. The ally can speak to the entity with you and will always let you know what it thinks is happening.

Outcome

You should encounter an imaginal entity with which you dialogue. After speaking with it for some time, you should experience an energy exchange between the entity and the ally and witness a gradual process of change within the ally. Keep working with this practice until you feel you have accomplished these goals.

Epilogue: Conclusion

I have presented practices extending from the beginning of ally work until far along the path. Not everyone will care to do all the practices, but I hope most of you will find some of them useful in the pursuit of relationship with the ally. I have tried to keep the focus on experiential practices but have included enough theory to give the you some idea of where the practices fit in the overall perspective of ally work. In future works I shall elaborate on the theory of the union with the ally in greater detail. When you experiment with the practices, you can expect to experience your own union with the ally in your own way. You may also find it possible to create your own practices based on the ones presented here. On the other hand, you may reap great benefits from spending much time on mastering just one practice.

It would be ideal if you were able to find a teacher to work with as you practice, but this is not always possible.

At the very least, you should ask a friend or spouse to work with you as you practice. This could mean that they practice as well, but it might simply mean that they tell you if they sense something is wrong. It is always advisable to have someone to give you feedback because if you have gone wrong, you might not know it.

I have taught these practices for many years and have never met anyone who has lost their way using them. But everyone needs an anchor in the outer world and it is a good idea not to practice until you feel you have found one.

How far your travel on the road of ally work and how much success you enjoy is ultimately up to you. Develop a steady and regular practice and keep at it no matter what difficulties you face, and sooner or later you will find your ally. Once you do, you may journey with it in trust and love, but never forget that however deeply you relate to the ally, it remains forever the untamed dragon.

Notes

1. William C. Chittick, *Imaginal Worlds* (Albany: State University of New York Press, 1994), p. 152.

2. Henry Corbin, *The Man of Light in Iranian Sufism*, Nancy Pearson, trans. (New Lebanon, NY: Omega Publications, 1994), p. 20.

3. Henry Corbin, *Avicenna and the Visionary Recital*, Bollingen Series LXVI (Princeton: Princeton University Press, 1988), p. 77.

4. William Chittick, *The Self-disclosure of God* (Albany: State University of New York Press, 1998), p. 332.

5. Chittick, *The Self-disclosure of God*, p. 333.

6. *Ibid.*

7. Quoted in Moshe Idel, *Kabbalah: New Perspectives* (New Haven: Yale University Press, 1988), p. 106.

8. Morienus, *A Testament of Alchemy*, Lee Stavenhagen, ed. (Hanover, NH: Brandeis University Press/University Press of New England, 1974), p. 37.

9. C. G. Jung, *Mysterium Coniunctionis,* The Collected Works of C. G. Jung vol. 14 *Mysterium Coniunctionis*, R.F.C. Hull, trans., Bollingen Series XX (Princeton: Princeton University Press, 1970), ¶ 180.

10. Idel, *Kabbalah: New Perspectives*, p. 103.

11. Salomon Trismosin, *Splendor Solis,* Joscelyn Godwin, trans. (Grand Rapids, MI: Phanes Press, 1991), p. 21.

12. C. G. Jung, The Collected Works of C. G. Jung, vol. 12: *Psychology and Alchemy*, R.F.C. Hull, trans., Bollingen Series XX, (Princeton: Princeton University Press, 1969) ¶ 390.

13. "The Golden Tripod," Michael Maier, ed., in *The Hermetic Museum*, Arthur Edward Waite, ed. (York Beach, ME: Samuel Weiser, 1991) p. 343.

14. John Pordage, *Philosophisches Send-Schreiben,* quoted in Johannes Fabricus, *Alchemy* (London: Diamond Books, 1989), p. 190.

15. Basil Valentine, *His Triumphant Chariot of Antimony,* L. G. Kelly, ed. English Renaissance Hermeticism, vol. 3, Garland Reference Library of the Humanities, vol. 1242 (New York: Garland Publishing, 1990), p. 19.

16. Nicholas Flammel, *Alchemical Hieroglyphics* (Berkeley Heights, CA: Heptangle Books, 1980), p. 20.

17. Jeffrey Raff, *Jung and the Alchemical Imagination* (Berwick, ME: Nicolas-Hays, 2000).

18. Giovanni Battista Nazari, *Three Dreams on the Transmutation of Metals,* Doug Skinner, trans. Magnum Opus Heremetic Sourceworks No. 27 (Glasgow: Adam McLean, n.d.), p. 52.

19. C. G. Jung, *Memories, Dreams, Reflections,* Aniela Jaffé, ed. (New York: Vintage Books, 1963), p. 183.

20. *Ibid.*

21. *Hermetica,* Brian P. Copenhaver, trans. (Cambridge, UK: Cambridge University Press, 1996), p. 1.

22. Corbin, *The Man of Light in Iranian Sufism,* pp. 75ff.

23. *Hermetica,* p. 41.

24. Rumi, *The Book of Love* Cole Barks, trans. (San Francisco: Harper, 2003), p. 41.

25. *The Book of Lambspring,* in *The Hermetic Museum,* p. 294.

26. There are dozens of translations of *The Emerald Tablet.* See, for example, Stanislas Klossowski De Rola, *Alchemy* (New York: Bounty Books, n.d.), p. 15.

27. Jacques Tesson, *The Green Lion,* Luc Velleneuve, trans. Hermetic Research Series no. 17 (Glasgow: Adam Mclean, 2003), p. 48.

28. Georg Ernst Stahl, *The Philosopher's Stone* (Glasgow: Adam Mclean, n.d.), p. 13.

29. Flammel, *Alchemical Hieroglyphics,* p. 84.

Bibliography

"The Book of Lambspring." In *The Hermetic Museum*. Arthur Edward Waite, ed. York Beach, ME: Samuel Weiser, 1994.

Chittick, William C. *Imaginal Worlds*. Albany: State University of New York Press, 1994.

————. *The Self-disclosure of God*. Albany: State University of New York Press, 1998.

Copenhaver, Brian P., trans. *Hermetica*. Cambridge: Cambridge University Press, 1996.

Corbin, Henry. *Avicenna and the Visionary Recital*, Bollingen Series LXVI. Princeton: Princeton University Press 1988.

————. *The Man of Light in Iranian Sufism*. Nancy Pearson, trans. New Lebanon, NY: Omega Publications, 1980.

The Emerald Tablet. In Klossowski de Rola, Stanizlas. *Alchemy*. New York: Bounty books, n.d.

Flammel, Nicholas. *Alchemical Hieroglyphs.* Berkeley Heights, CA: Heptangle Books, 1980.

Halevi, Z'ev ben Shimon. *The Way of Kabbalah.* London: Rider, 1976.

Idel, Moshe. *Kabbalah: New Perspectives.* New Haven: Yale University Press, 1988.

Jung, C. G. *The Collected Works of C. G. Jung,* vol. 14: *Mysterium Coniunctionis.* R.F.C. Hull, trans. Bollingen Series XX. Princeton: Princeton University Press 1970.

———. *The Collected Works of C. G. Jung,* vol. 12: *Psychology and Alchemy,* Bollingen Series XX. Princeton: Princeton University Press 1969.

———. *Memories, Dreams, Reflections.* George and Clara Winston, trans. Aniela Jaffé, ed. New York: Vintage, 1963.

Maier, Michael, ed. "The Golden Tripod." In *The Hermetic Museum.* Arthur Edward Waite, ed. York Beach, ME: Samuel Weiser, 1991.

Morienus. *A Testament of Alchemy.* Hanover, NH: Brandeis University Press/University Press of New England 1974.

Nazari, Giovanni Battista. *Three Dreams on the Transmutation of Metals.* Doug Skinner, trans. Magnum Opus Hermetic Sourceworks no. 27. Glasgow: Adam McLean, n.d.

Pordage, John. *Philosophisches Send-Schreiben.* Quoted in Johannes Fabricus. *Alchemy.* London: Diamond Books, 1989.

Raff, Jeffrey. *Jung and the Alchemical Imagination.* Berwick, ME: Nicolas-Hays, 2000.

Rumi. *The Book of Love.* Coleman Barks, trans. San Francisco: Harper, 2003.

Stahl, Georg Ernst. *The Philosopher's Stone.* Glasgow: Adam McLean, n.d.

Tesson, Jacques. *The Green Lion.* Luc Velleneuve, trans. Hermetic Research Series no. 17. Glasgow: Adam McLean, 2003.

Trismosin, Solomon. *Splendor Solis.* Joscelyn Godwin, trans. Grand Rapids, MI: Phanes Press, 1991.

Valentine, Basil. *His Triumphant Chariot of Antimony.* L. G. Kelly, ed. English Renaissance Hermeticism vol. 3, Garland Reference Library of the Humanities, vol. 1242. New York: Garland Publishing, 1990.

Index

About the Author

Jeffrey Raff received his B.A. from Bates College, a Master's in Psychology from the New School for Social Research, and a Ph.D. in Psychology from the Union Graduate School. He graduated as a diplomate from the C. G. Jung Institute in Zurich. He has had a private practice in Littleton, Colorado, since 1976, and teaches classes, seminars, and workshops on Jungian psychology and alchemy all over the country. Readers may contact Dr. Raff at his Web site http://www.jeffraff.com.